Marcowitz, Hal
The 1960s

973.62
MAR

Understanding
American History

The 1960s

Hal Marcovitz

Bruno Leone
Series Consultant

ReferencePoint
Press®

San Diego, CA

© 2013 ReferencePoint Press, Inc.
Printed in the United States

For more information, contact:
ReferencePoint Press, Inc.
PO Box 27779
San Diego, CA 92198
www.ReferencePointPress.com

LIBRARY OF CONGRESS CATALOGING-IN-PUBLICATION DATA

Marcovitz, Hal.
   The 1960s / by Hal Marcovitz.
      p. cm. -- (Understanding American history series)
   Includes bibliographical references and index.
   ISBN-13: 978-1-60152-494-2 (hardback)
   ISBN-10: 1-60152-494-3 (hardback)
   1. United States--History--1961-1969--Juvenile literature. 2. United States--Social conditions--1960-1980--Juvenile literature. 3. United States--Social life and customs--1945-1970--Juvenile literature. I. Title. II. Title: Nineteen sixties.
   E839.M368 2013
   973.92--dc23
                                                                                     2012032157

Contents

Foreword

America's Puritan ancestors—convinced that their adopted country was blessed by God and would eventually rise to worldwide prominence—proclaimed their new homeland the shining "city upon a hill." The nation that developed since those first hopeful words were uttered has clearly achieved prominence on the world stage and it has had many shining moments but its history is not without flaws. The history of the United States is a virtual patchwork of achievements and blemishes. For example, America was originally founded as a New World haven from the tyranny and persecution prevalent in many parts of the Old World. Yet the colonial and federal governments in America took little or no action against the use of slave labor by the southern states until the 1860s, when a civil war was fought to eliminate slavery and preserve the federal union.

In the decades before and after the Civil War, the United States underwent a period of massive territorial expansion; through a combination of purchase, annexation, and war, its east–west borders stretched from the Atlantic to the Pacific Oceans. During this time, the Industrial Revolution that began in eighteenth-century Europe found its way to America, where it was responsible for considerable growth of the national economy. The United States was now proudly able to take its place in the Western Hemisphere's community of nations as a worthy economic and technological partner. Yet America also chose to join the major western European powers in a race to acquire colonial empires in Africa, Asia, and the islands of the Caribbean and South Pacific. In this scramble for empire, foreign territories were often peacefully annexed but military force was readily used when needed, as in the Philippines during the Spanish-American War of 1898.

Toward the end of the nineteenth century and concurrent with America's ambitions to acquire colonies, its vast frontier and expanding industrial base provided both land and jobs for a new and ever-growing wave of immigrants from southern and eastern Europe. Although America had always encouraged immigration, these newcomers—Italians, Greeks, and eastern European Jews, among others—were seen as different from the vast majority of earlier immigrants, most of whom were from northern and western Europe. The presence of these newcomers was treated as a matter of growing concern, which in time evolved into intense opposition. Congress boldly and with calculated prejudice set out to create a barrier to curtail the influx of unwanted nationalities and ethnic groups to America's shores. The outcome was the National Origins Act, passed in 1924. That law severely reduced immigration to the United States from southern and eastern Europe. Ironically, while this was happening, the Statue of Liberty stood in New York Harbor as a visible and symbolic beacon lighting the way for people of *all* nationalities and ethnicities seeking sanctuary in America.

Unquestionably, the history of the United States has not always mirrored that radiant beacon touted by the early settlers. As often happens, reality and dreams tend to move in divergent directions. However, the story of America also reveals a people who have frequently extended a helping hand to a weary world and who have displayed a ready willingness—supported by a flexible federal constitution—to take deliberate and effective steps to correct injustices, past and present. America's private and public philanthropy directed toward other countries during times of natural disasters (such as the contributions of financial and human resources to assist Haiti following the January 2010, earthquake) and the legal right to adopt amendments to the US Constitution (including the Thirteenth Amendment freeing the slaves and the Nineteenth Amendment granting women the right to vote) are examples of the nation's generosity and willingness to acknowledge and reverse wrongs.

With objectivity and candor, the titles selected for the Understanding American History series portray the many sides of America, depicting both its shining moments and its darker hours. The series strives to help readers achieve a wider understanding and appreciation of the American experience and to encourage further investigation into America's evolving character and founding principles.

Important Events of the 1960s

1960

To call attention to the South's racist Jim Crow laws, four African American men take seats at a whites-only lunch counter in Greensboro, North Carolina, and, as expected, are refused service. Massachusetts senator John F. Kennedy faces Vice President Richard M. Nixon in the first televised presidential debate; Kennedy's strong showing in the debate helps him upset Nixon in the November presidential election.

1963

Author Betty Friedan publishes *The Feminine Mystique,* reporting that many American women want careers and are not satisfied with their roles as stay-at-home wives and mothers. On November 22, while riding in a motorcade in Dallas, Texas, President John F. Kennedy is shot and killed by Lee Harvey Oswald.

1960   1961   1962   1963   1964

1961

In April a CIA-sponsored invasion of Cuba staged by Cuban exiles is thwarted at the Bay of Pigs. On May 5 astronaut Alan B. Shepard Jr. becomes the first American launched into space. Shepard's accomplishment prompts a national commitment to space travel by the American people.

1964

On February 9 the Beatles make the first of three appearances on *The Ed Sullivan Show.* Some 73 million Americans tune in to watch the performance of the Fab Four. On August 7 Congress passes the Gulf of Tonkin Resolution, empowering President Johnson to use military force to stem Communist aggression in South Vietnam.

1962

After detecting nuclear weapons based in Cuba by the Soviet Union, Kennedy orders a blockade of the island and demands the Soviets withdraw their missiles. For thirteen days in October the United States and Soviet Union teeter on the edge of nuclear warfare, until the Soviets back down and remove the missiles.

1965

President Lyndon B. Johnson orders a massive buildup of troops into South Vietnam; by December some two hundred thousand US troops are engaged in combat in Southeast Asia.

1967

On January 27 astronauts Gus Grissom, Ed White, and Roger Chaffee die in a fire while locked in an Apollo space capsule as it sits on its launchpad. The tragedy delays America's plans for a moon mission by a year and a half as engineers work to make the capsule safer.

1968

In January, North Vietnamese troops launch the Tet Offensive, a massive military invasion of South Vietnam. Civil rights leader Martin Luther King Jr. is assassinated on April 4 in Memphis, Tennessee. Senator Robert F. Kennedy is assassinated on June 5 in Los Angeles, California. In August antiwar rioters disrupt the Democratic National Convention in Chicago, Illinois; later in the year, Republican Richard M. Nixon is elected president.

1965   1966   1967   1968   1969

1966

In Vietnam the bombing campaign known as Operation Rolling Thunder is in full force. Each month, American bombers stage seven thousand raids on military targets as well as roads and bridges in North Vietnam.

1969

On July 20 American astronaut Neil Armstrong takes his first step on the lunar surface. In August a half-million young people gather at a farm near Woodstock, New York, to attend a rock festival; activists and performers use the stage to voice their opposition to the Vietnam War.

The Defining Characteristics of the 1960s

William D. Ehrhart had spent twelve months in Vietnam and had one month left to serve "in country" under the terms of his enlistment in the US Marines. During his tour he participated in numerous firefights, slept in boggy jungles, endured long patrols in searing heat, and yet had survived. But now with just a month left, Ehrhart felt frightened. "Guys got [killed] in their first few months because they simply hadn't yet learned enough to avoid getting it," Ehrhart says. "Guys got it in their last few months because they got stupid. They couldn't suppress just a little longer the intoxicating illusion that they were actually going to get out of the game ahead."[1]

Ehrhart survived the Vietnam War and returned home in 1968—bitter and feeling that he risked his life in an unwinnable conflict. Moreover, Ehrhart felt no measure of pride in his duty, believing America had no business interfering in the internal problems of a country half a world away. Says Ehrhart,

> There is an implicit but sacred bargain struck between those who ask others to put their lives at risk and those who do the risking. It goes like this: I will give you my life to do with what you will so long as your cause is worthy of my sacrifice. I accepted that bargain willingly, proudly, because those who put me at risk assured me and my country that the cause was indeed

worthy. During the long, painful 13 months I fought in Vietnam, however, I became less and less confident that I and my government knew what we were doing.[2]

Era of Change

At home, doubts about the war and outright opposition to it grew among millions of Americans. Many took to the streets, staging boisterous demonstrations that often ended in clashes with police. The debate over the nation's involvement in Vietnam often turned tumultuous, but there were many other controversies during the era that sparked public protest, leading to deep divisions among the American people. During the 1960s African Americans, women, and others fought for equal

Demonstrators take to the streets in 1968 to protest US involvement in the Vietnam War. The war and the rising tide of opposition to it provided the backdrop for many of the other political and cultural changes that took place during the 1960s.

rights. Young people born in the years following World War II grew into teenagers and young adults during the 1960s. Many sought to break with the staid conventions of the past and escape the influence of their parents and political leaders.

The rebellion of the 1960s took many forms: Many young people rebelled by simply growing their hair long and blasting rock 'n' roll music on their stereos; others by experimenting with marijuana and harder drugs. Many young men of draft age fled America, most moving to Canada to wait out the war. Others defiantly burned their draft cards, which classified their eligibility for conscription into the armed services. Many young people joined the "free love" movement, rebelliously practicing promiscuous behavior because, at the time, society frowned on couples having sex out of wedlock. Many young people dropped out of society, joining communes where they raised and shared their food but also each other's drugs and sexual partners.

Looking back, those who came of age in the 1960s believe their rebellion bore fruit. During the 1960s the rights of African Americans and members of other minority groups were recognized under law. So were the rights of women. And largely because of the antiwar demonstrations, political leaders finally concluded that the American people would no longer support a long and bloody foreign conflict whose purpose had no clear and direct impact on American security. The 1960s radical leader Abbie Hoffman may have summed it up best when he said, "Sure, we were young. We were arrogant. We were ridiculous. There were excesses. We were brash. We were foolish. But we were right."[3]

Chapter 1

What Conditions Led to the 1960s?

Kathleen Casey was born one second past midnight on January 1, 1946. As such, the birth of the little girl from Pennsauken, New Jersey, was the first in what eventually became known as the "baby boom"—the 76 million Americans born in a twenty-year period following World War II. Many of their fathers were veterans who had returned home from the war, married their sweethearts, and settled down to life in postwar America. A large number of the children of these marriages grew into teenagers and young adults during the 1960s.

It would be the baby boomers who would find themselves most affected by the turbulent 1960s. They marched for civil rights and free speech, fought in Vietnam, and demanded cultural changes—a sharp break from the conservative culture forged by their parents. "We had a great, great ride," says Casey. "We had opportunities like no other generation. And we had fun. We dared."[4]

The decades preceding the 1960s set the stage for the volatility and changes to come. "The pace of the Fifties seemed slower, more languid," writes author David Halberstam in his book *The Fifties*. "The Fifties appear to be an orderly era, one with a minimum of social dissent. Photographs from the period tend to show people who dressed carefully; men in suits, ties, and—when outdoors—hats; the women with their hair in modified page-boys, pert and upbeat. Young people seemed, more than anything else, 'square' and largely accepting of the social covenants."[5] But below this gentle surface lurked the voices of dissent that, as the 1960s arrived, refused to remain silent any longer. "Social ferment," Halberstam writes, "was beginning just beneath this placid surface."[6]

The First Superpower

The baby boomers came of age as America was taking on a new role in the international community. As the countries of Europe and Asia rebuilt their economies and societies in the years following World War II, America assumed the role of a superpower and, therefore, the strongest nation on the planet. But American supremacy would soon be challenged by the Soviet Union, which aimed to spread its influence throughout the world. The Soviet Union was ruled by an authoritarian Communist regime that sought to control all facets of life: political, economic, and social. Americans believed they had much to fear from communism. At home, such agitators as US senator Joseph McCarthy and members of the US House Un-American Activities Committee stirred up fears of Communist infiltration of American institutions, including the government. In other corners of the world the Communist regimes in the Soviet Union and China sponsored revolutions or engaged in outright occupations.

During the late 1940s and throughout the 1950s, many eastern European countries, including East Germany, Poland, Czechoslovakia, Bulgaria, and Romania, became "satellite" countries of the Soviet Union—their governments completely under control of the Communist leadership in Moscow. Meanwhile, fears of a Communist Chinese–sponsored takeover in Korea sparked the Korean War in 1950. American troops arrived that year to shore up the democratically elected government of South Korea and spent the next three years fighting Communist troops from North Korea—as well as Chinese troops who joined the battle. A cease-fire was finally declared in 1954 with the two sides mired in a stalemate. More than fifty thousand American soldiers died in Korea, and another hundred thousand were wounded in action. Many Americans had made the ultimate sacrifice to preserve democracy in Korea, and yet the conflict resolved little.

The Cold War

As the Soviets dominated eastern Europe and the Chinese spread their influence throughout Asia, the prospect of nuclear war hovered in the background. World War II ended in 1945 when American planes dropped atomic bombs on the Japanese cities of Hiroshima and Naga-saki, killing some two hundred thousand people. Throughout the 1950s America continued expanding its nuclear arsenal, developing even more devastating bombs as well as intercontinental ballistic missiles (ICBMs)

Atomic Blasts and Bathing Suits

Atomic tests ramped up the Cold War and prompted many people to dig backyard fallout shelters. But they also worked wonders for the women's swimwear industry.

In 1946 two French designers, working independently, developed designs for two-piece bathing suits. One designer, Jacques Heim, named his bathing suit *l'Atome* (in English, the atom) because, he boasted, it was as small as the smallest particle known to science. His rival, Louis Réard, took inspiration from an atomic test staged by the American military at Bikini, an atoll in a group of islands in the South Pacific. Réard named his suit "the bikini," which proved to be the more popular name among shoppers.

During the 1940s and much of the 1950s bikinis were regarded as daring beachwear, but the style took off after French movie star Brigitte Bardot wore one in the 1956 film *And God Created Woman*. By the 1960s bikinis were standard at most American beaches. Wrote *Ebony* magazine in 1964, "The bikini remains the most welcome . . . of summer delights."

As for the Bikini atoll, atomic tests continued there until 1958. The islands remain uninhabitable more than fifty years later due to lingering radiation from the tests.

Ebony, "Swimsuits: From the 'Bare' to the 'Covered Up,'" February 1964, p. 107.

A nuclear device is detonated during testing in 1951 at Nevada's Yucca Flat. The United States and Soviet Union devoted enormous sums of money to development of nuclear weapons during the Cold War.

that could deliver the weapons to targets thousands of miles away. Indeed, ICBMs launched from underground silos in South Dakota or Kansas could reach cities in the Soviet Union in a matter of minutes.

Meanwhile, newsreel cameras recorded the so-called "A-tests" of the era as the military staged atomic bomb explosions in such places as Eniwetok, an atoll in a group of small islands in the South Pacific, and Yucca Flat, a barren region of Nevada. Cameras positioned miles away from ground zero recorded the devastating power of the explosions as well as the "mushroom" clouds that rose high into the sky. Frightened by those images and the news that the Soviets were developing their own atomic weapons, many Americans built backyard fallout shelters—underground safe havens, stocked with food and water. In the event of a Soviet attack, these Americans hoped to retreat to their shelters to escape the blast and avoid breathing the deadly radioactive dust that rains down from the sky following the detonation of an atomic bomb. Meanwhile, school children were shown films explaining how to "duck and cover" during an atomic attack. To escape the glass shards from their classroom windows that would shoot toward them during the blasts, students were advised to hide under their desks.

In the minds of many Americans, communism represented a major threat to democratic principles and America itself. This era marked the start of the Cold War—decades of icy relations between the United States and Soviet Union when both countries ramped up their nuclear arsenals while aiming to spread their influence to the remainder of the world. Throughout the years of the Cold War, America and the Soviet Union regarded each other as enemies, yet both countries avoided direct military conflict.

Why Was It Called the "Cold War"?

The term "Cold War" was coined by Bernard Baruch, a millionaire financier and adviser to several presidents from Woodrow Wilson to Harry S. Truman. Baruch labeled the icy relations between the United States and Soviet Union the "Cold War" during a speech before the South Carolina House of Representatives, where his portrait was being unveiled. A South Carolina native, Baruch told the legislators in the April 16, 1947, speech, "Let us not be deceived. We are today in the midst of a Cold War. Our enemies are to be found abroad and at home. Let us never forget this: Our unrest is the heart of their success."

Later that year Baruch's friend, *New York Herald Tribune* columnist Walter Lippmann, used the term in his column. The phrase was soon used widely by other journalists and commentators.

Quoted in Andrew Glass, "Bernard Baruch Coins the Term 'Cold War,' April 16, 1947," *Politico*, April 16, 2010. www.politico.com.

Americans Arrive in Vietnam

One place where the Cold War had turned hot was in a tiny Asian country of which most Americans knew little during the 1950s. For more than a century, the people of the Southeast Asian nation of Vietnam had struggled to win their independence from French and Japanese occupiers. Following World War II France tried to reassert its colonial rule over Vietnam, but a guerilla force known as the Vietminh fought relentlessly against the occupiers. In 1954 the Vietminh scored a decisive victory against the French army in a battle near the city of Dien Bien Phu in northwestern Vietnam.

The Vietminh were led by a Communist, Ho Chi Minh, and received arms and aid from the Communist regime in China. Soon after the Vietminh victory, Vietnam was granted its independence at a peace conference in Geneva, Switzerland. However, one significant condition was attached to Vietnamese independence: Under the terms of the treaty, Vietnamese territory north of the seventeenth parallel of latitude would be turned over to Ho and his Communist regime, while the South would remain under the control of a former Vietnamese emperor, Bao Dai, who had administered the Vietnamese puppet government under the French. Under the terms of the treaty, elections would be held in 1956 to determine the future of the country. Ho grudgingly accepted the terms but felt confident he could unite the country during the 1956 elections.

By 1955 the South came under the leadership of Ngo Dinh Diem, the prime minister appointed by Bao. Diem soon announced the South would not participate in the coming unification election. Instead, he declared the independence of the South, naming it the Republic of Vietnam (or, more familiarly to Americans, South Vietnam). Diem's decision sparked a resumption of war between South Vietnam and the Communist North, now known as the Democratic Republic of Vietnam (or, to Americans, North Vietnam). President Dwight D. Eisenhower pledged military support to Diem, and in 1955 the first arms and supplies as well as the first American military advisers arrived in the South Vietnamese capital of Saigon to help train the South Vietnamese army. Over the coming years, American involvement in Vietnam would steadily increase.

Window into the World

To the young American baby boomers growing up in the 1950s, these events were of little interest. The children of the 1950s rushed home from school each day to watch *The Mickey Mouse Club* on TV. Produced by the studio headed by movie animator Walt Disney, *The Mickey Mouse Club* featured cartoons and action-packed serials featuring the adventures of teenage sleuths known as the Hardy Boys. It also presented elaborate song and dance numbers performed by the Mouseketeers, young people whose faces and names became familiar

to millions of young fans. Before watching the show, dedicated viewers were sure to don their mouse ears. Other popular children's shows
of the era included *Howdy Doody*, which featured a marionette with
a quick wit, and another puppet show, *Kukla, Fran and Ollie*. Meanwhile, the Lone Ranger made his first appearance on American TV
during the 1950s.

Indeed, television had exploded as a medium of entertainment
in the 1950s, but it also became an important source of news. In
1946 there were fewer than ten thousand TV sets in American
homes; in 1960 televisions could be found in 58 million American
homes, or about 90 percent of American households. Throughout
the 1950s and 1960s, television would emerge as an important window into the world for millions of Americans who could see news-
worthy events unfold live—albeit, well into the 1960s, mostly in
black and white.

Television would play an important role in heightening the ten-
sions of the Cold War. On the one hand, the TV networks of the era
often aired dramas that focused on espionage, as fearless American
agents uncovered Communist plots to steal atomic secrets or otherwise undermine American society. For example, in 1953 an episode
of the series *Suspense* featured a plot by foreign agents, disguised
as American businessmen, attempting to smuggle technology to the
Soviet Union. That same year an episode of *Fireside Theater* featured
an American soldier, captured by the North Koreans, who agrees to
turn traitor.

On the other hand, television also proved itself to be a power-
ful medium in exposing the falsehoods and propaganda promoted by
people such as Senator Joseph McCarthy, who conducted a witch hunt
for suspected Communists. During the so-called "Army-McCarthy"
hearings of 1954, TV networks provided Americans with live coverage of the congressional hearings that McCarthy hoped would expose
Communist infiltrators in the American military. Instead, the hearings
exposed McCarthy as a liar and charlatan. Defending the army during
the hearings was prominent Boston attorney Joseph N. Welch. In a

landmark moment during the hearings, McCarthy suggested that an attorney in Welch's firm harbored Communist sympathies. Welch angrily responded, "Until this moment, senator, I think I never gauged your cruelty or recklessness. . . . Have you no sense of decency, sir, at long last? Have you left no sense of decency?"[7] Welsh's accusation prompted the packed hearing room gallery to erupt in applause. A dumbstruck McCarthy then turned to his committee's lawyer and mumbled, "What happened?"[8]

Rock 'n' Roll Arrives

One news story that dominated the newspaper headlines as well as the new TV news broadcasts during the 1950s was unrest by African Americans in the South. In 1954 the US Supreme Court declared school segregation illegal in the *Brown v. Board of Education* case. Despite the Supreme Court ruling, desegregation did not happen overnight because many southern politicians vowed to fight on. Perhaps the most flagrant challenge to the Supreme Court ruling occurred in 1957 when Arkansas governor Orval Faubus called out his state's National Guard to prevent nine black students from attending Little Rock High School. Eisenhower responded by sending federal troops to ensure the students would be admitted to school.

Stories about the rise of communism in Southeast Asia or the struggles of African Americans in the southern states may have been dominating the airwaves of TV and radio broadcasts, but news about these grim events often competed for airtime with a new wave of entertainment that emerged in the 1950s. By the late 1950s the first boomers were reaching their teenage years and, as their horrified parents could attest, many of their children were developing a shocking taste in music.

In 1951 Cleveland, Ohio, disc jockey Alan Freed started playing a new sound for his listeners—it was called "rock 'n' roll." Soon, early stars such as Bill Haley and the Comets, Buddy Holly, Carl Perkins, Jerry Lee Lewis, and Roy Orbison refined the sound. In 1954 Elvis Presley, a young singer from Tupelo, Mississippi, released his

Musical tastes took a turn in the 1950s as the first wave of baby boomers began rocking to the sounds of musicians such as Jerry Lee Lewis, Buddy Holly, and Elvis Presley (pictured in 1956). Rock 'n' roll became an international sensation, fueled by the likes of the Beatles and the Rolling Stones.

first single, "Red, Hot and Blue," which skyrocketed to the top of the charts and turned Presley into a star.

Rock 'n' roll also appealed to fans outside the United States. In 1957 teenager John Lennon from Liverpool, England, formed his first band, which he named the Black Jacks. The band would undergo many changes in personnel and perform under different names until finally,

Lennon and the others settled on the Quarrymen. By then another teenager from Liverpool, Paul McCartney, had joined the band.

By 1960 the group had found its way to Hamburg, Germany, where Lennon, McCartney, and the others achieved modest success playing in the city's nightclubs. By then the band had undergone a few more name changes and was now known as the Beatles. Meanwhile, as the Beatles were playing Hamburg nightclubs, another young English singer, Michael Phillip Jagger—Mick to his friends—entered the London School of Economics, but his love for rock 'n' roll music would soon convince him to drop out and form his own band.

Changes on the Horizon

As the 1950s drew to a close, America and the rest of the world were on the brink of change. In Vietnam, hostilities continued to escalate. Communists were making gains in other countries as well—particularly on the island nation of Cuba, less than one hundred miles from Florida. Meanwhile, in the southern states, African Americans pushed for equality and their efforts were paying off. A clear victory for equality could be found in the Montgomery bus boycott, which commenced in 1955 when a black woman, Rosa Parks, was jailed in Montgomery, Alabama, for refusing to give up her seat to a white rider on a public bus. The incident led to a yearlong boycott of the Montgomery public transit system by African American riders, which dealt a devastating economic blow to the city's bus company. Moreover, the boycott led to the emergence of the Reverend Martin Luther King Jr. as the nation's most prominent civil rights leader as he became the spiritual as well as tactical leader of the boycott. During the boycott, leaders of the movement were harassed, bullied, roughed up, and jailed. And yet they persevered. "In unity and violence the blacks found new strength, particularly as the nation began to take notice," says Halberstam. "Things that had for so long terrified them—the idea of being arrested and spending the night in prison, for example, became a badge of honor. Their purpose now was greater than their terror."[9] Finally, after a year, the city's bus company relented and agreed to permit blacks to choose their own seats on the buses.

More change was on the horizon. As the 1960 presidential election approached, Massachusetts senator John F. Kennedy, a Catholic, emerged as a leading candidate, presenting the clear possibility that Americans would elect their first president from a non-Protestant faith. Of all Americans, though, the baby boomers would be most affected by the changes that were coming. As folk singer Bob Dylan warned parents in his 1963 song, "The Times They Are A-Changin," it was time for them to step aside, their sons and daughters were now "beyond your command."[10]

Chapter 2

The Pursuit of American Exceptionalism

In the twenty-first century, television plays a big role in presidential politics: Candidates debate numerous times in front of national TV audiences while network news cameras follow them as they cross the country seeking votes. Television's devotion to presidential politics can arguably be traced back to September 26, 1960, when John F. Kennedy, the Democratic nominee, faced Vice President Richard M. Nixon, the Republican nominee, in the nation's first televised presidential debate. Prior to the debate Kennedy was regarded as the underdog in the election. But the debate raised his status among the American people, making him a viable contender for the presidency.

The debate was televised from a TV studio in Chicago. Kennedy spent the day relaxing with aides on the roof of his hotel, going over note cards to prep for the questions that would be posed by a panel of journalists. In contrast, Nixon spent a busy day attending a series of campaign events. Moreover, due to a recent hospitalization, Nixon appeared pale and underweight. Fearing the harsh glare of the television lights, Nixon wore a heavy layer of pancake makeup during the debate. Nevertheless, his five-o'clock shadow still showed through, and beads of sweat formed under his nose and on his chin, giving his face an unappealing appearance on the TV screens of those who watched the telecast. Among them was Nixon aide Herb Klein, who later recalled his private reaction was, "Fire the make-up man."[11]

Kennedy eschewed makeup, preferring instead to show off the tan he had received on the hotel roof that afternoon. When the Massachusetts senator arrived at the TV studio, he was well rested and clear-headed. On TV Kennedy appeared younger, healthier, more vibrant, and certainly more telegenic than Nixon, and that is what impressed a majority of the 74 million viewers who watched the debate in their living rooms at home. Writes journalist Theodore H. White, "It is impossible to look again at the still photographs of Nixon in his ordeal and to recollect the circumstances without utmost sympathy. For everything that could have gone wrong that night went wrong."[12]

The New Frontier

Six weeks later Nixon lost the election to Kennedy by a narrow margin. When Kennedy was inaugurated in January 1961, he promised a "New Frontier"—an array of social programs that would eradicate poverty, help bring equality to the races, promote international peace, and sponsor new advancements in science. These were elements of "American exceptionalism": the concept that America holds a unique place in the world; that due to the nation's democratic ideals and personal liberties, Americans could be world leaders in all facets of culture and society.

Kennedy was a firm believer in American exceptionalism. By the time of his inauguration, many of the nation's leaders were less sure of America's role in the world. Indeed, when Kennedy took the oath of office on January 20, 1961, America had already fallen behind in the space race. By today's standards, the launch of the satellite known as *Sputnik* would hardly be regarded as a significant achievement. *Sputnik*—a Russian word that roughly translates to "traveling companion"—weighed just 183.6 pounds (83.3kg) and measured a mere 22.8 inches (57.9cm) in diameter. *Sputnik*'s lone function as it orbited Earth was to emit a beep that could be tracked by radio receivers on the ground.

And yet, when the satellite was launched on October 5, 1957, it marked a milestone in both science and the Cold War. American scientists and engineers had, for years, been planning the launch of an artificial satellite into Earth's orbit with an eye toward eventually sending astronauts into space. But now the Soviets had reached space first. US political leaders were shocked. They feared the Soviets held the edge in the race for space and, in time, would gain the expertise to place nuclear weapons in orbit. Such weapons, it was believed, would make it possible for the Soviet Union to attack American cities. "It cannot

At his January 1961 inauguration, President John F. Kennedy speaks to the nation from the steps of the Capitol. Kennedy's "New Frontier" programs were aimed at eradicating poverty, bringing racial equality, and sponsoring advances in science.

S ome of the scientists and engineers responsible for designing American rockets during the 1960s first used their talents to help Nazi Germany build rockets to bomb London and other cities during World War II. Led by engineer Wernher von Braun, they were responsible for developing the dreaded V2 rocket, three thousand of which rained down on cities in Great Britain and Belgium starting in 1944. The "V" stood for *Vergeltungswaffe* (in English, "vengeance craft.")

In 1945, as American troops advanced toward Germany, von Braun and many of his fellow rocket scientists allowed themselves to be captured and spirited back to America in a mission known as Operation Paperclip. The mission was organized by US intelligence agents who realized the Germans' value in a postwar world where America would be in competition with the Soviet Union to develop weapons. The German scientists soon lent their expertise to the development of intercontinental ballistic missiles as well as the American space program.

be overemphasized that the survival of the free world—indeed, all the world—is caught up in the stakes,"[13] declared Representative John McCormack in 1959.

Project Mercury

The US government responded quickly to the launch of *Sputnik*. In early 1958 the first American satellite, *Explorer 1*, was launched into orbit. Meanwhile, resources were poured into the space program, which had been under the direction of the US Air Force as well as a number of civilian agencies. Later in 1958 Congress created the National Aeronautics and Space Administration (NASA) to lead the American space program. NASA immediately started recruiting the nation's top physicists, aeronautical engineers, and other scientists. Its goal was to develop the rockets that American politicians insisted the country would need if it expected to keep pace with the Soviets. Moreover, NASA started culling through the ranks of the best American military test pilots—seeking to build a corps of astronauts who would one day ride those rockets into space.

But despite the best efforts of NASA, the Soviets would once again prove their superiority in space science. On April 12, 1961, a Soviet rocket blasted into space, carrying cosmonaut Yuri Gagarin into orbit. As with *Sputnik*, the flight hardly proved the Soviets were in a position to dominate the heavens. Gagarin's capsule made a single orbit of Earth—he spent a mere 108 minutes in space. He reached an altitude of 187 miles (301km), high enough to propel him into orbit and achieve weightlessness. As the capsule hurtled toward Earth, Gagarin bailed out and parachuted to the ground: The Soviet engineers had not yet solved the problem of how to bring the capsule in for a soft landing. And yet, once again, American politicians fumed. Vice President Lyndon B. Johnson proclaimed that the Soviet manned space program could lead to Communist colonization of the moon and the planets. Said Johnson, "I do not think that this generation of Americans is willing to go to bed each night by the light of a communist moon."[14]

America took its first step toward catching up with the Soviets on May 5, 1961, when astronaut Alan B. Shepard Jr. was blasted into space as part of Project Mercury—NASA's first phase of its manned spaceflight program. Shepard's flight was suborbital—it lasted a mere fifteen minutes and only reached an altitude of 115 miles (185km). Shepard's capsule, however, made a soft landing; as the spacecraft fell to Earth, parachutes were released. This slowed the descent and allowed the capsule to splash down into the Atlantic Ocean where it was retrieved by a US Navy ship, with Shepard still aboard. "The only complaint I have," Shepard said, "was the flight was not long enough."[15]

Two Weeks in Space

Shepard's achievement thrilled the American people. He was immediately elevated to the status of a national hero and given a ticker tape parade in New York City. Moreover, based on the modest success of Shepard's flight, just three weeks later Kennedy stood before Congress and made this bold commitment to the American space program: "I believe that this nation should commit itself to achieving the goal, before this decade is out, of landing a man on the moon and returning him safely to Earth. No single space project in this period will be more impressive to mankind or more important for the long-range exploration of space. And none will be so difficult or expensive to accomplish."[16]

Five more Mercury missions would follow Shepard's flight, the most notable of which was the launch of *Friendship 7*, the space capsule carrying astronaut John Glenn into orbit. On February 20, 1962, Glenn's capsule made three orbits of Earth before splashing down safely into the Atlantic Ocean. This achievement—sending an American astronaut into Earth orbit—helped America catch up with the Soviets. Moreover, the success of Glenn's flight convinced many Americans that it would be possible to fulfill Kennedy's commitment—to reach the moon by the end of the decade.

The Mercury program ended on May 16, 1963, when astronaut Gordon Cooper's space capsule orbited Earth twenty-two times before splashing down in the Atlantic. Cooper spent thirty-four hours aloft—the first endurance test for the American space program. Two years later astronauts Gus Grissom and John Young flew the first of the ten manned missions, in each of which two astronauts orbited Earth, sitting side by side in a Gemini capsule. These missions were regarded as dress rehearsals for the coming flight to the moon. Gemini crews spent as long as two weeks in space. During the missions, crew members left the capsules to "walk" in space. They also practiced complicated docking maneuvers, linking craft to craft in mid orbit, which would be required for the moon missions. On November 15, 1966, the last Gemini capsule splashed down in the Atlantic Ocean after completing a five-day orbital mission. NASA engineers and the corps of astronauts now looked toward the commencement of Project Apollo and the flight to the moon.

"One Giant Leap"

Sadly, the lunar program would be marked by tragedy before the first in-flight test of the three-astronaut Apollo capsule. On January 27, 1967, astronauts Grissom, Ed White, and Roger Chaffee died in a fire while locked in the capsule as it sat on its launchpad. The three astronauts were participating in a test of the craft weeks before the first scheduled launch when, evidently, an electrical spark caused the pure oxygen atmosphere in the capsule to ignite. The accident not only took the lives of the astronauts but caused a year-and-a-half delay in the Apollo program as engineers worked to redesign the spacecraft to avoid similar catastrophes.

The Apollo flights commenced in 1968, first with an orbital mission and then, in December, a flight to the moon in which the three astronauts, Frank Borman, James Lovell, and William Anders, made the first manned spaceflight that escaped Earth's orbit. *Apollo 8* embarked on a one-week journey, circling the moon ten times before returning to Earth. The following May a second practice mission was staged, and then, on July 16, 1969, *Apollo 11* blasted off for the moon, carrying astronauts Neil Armstrong, Edwin "Buzz" Aldrin, and Michael Collins. After a four-day flight, the lunar landing craft *Eagle* separated from the Apollo capsule and descended to the moon. Carrying Armstrong and Aldrin, the capsule touched down in a sparse plain on the moon known as the Sea of Tranquility. At 4:18 p.m. eastern time on July 20, tens of millions of people worldwide, watching live coverage of the mission on TV or listening on their radios, heard Armstrong utter the first words spoken from the moon. Addressing NASA's mission control in Houston, Texas, Armstrong said, "Houston, Tranquility Base here. The *Eagle* has landed."[17]

More than seven hours later, at 10:45 p.m. eastern time, Armstrong opened the hatch of the *Eagle* and stepped onto a ladder. As he descended toward the lunar surface, he manipulated a lever that opened a shelf on which rested a remote TV camera. The camera focused on the astronaut as he descended the rungs. On Earth an estimated half-billion people watched the grainy black-and-white image of Armstrong

Astronaut Edwin "Buzz" Aldrin walks on the moon on July 20, 1969. He and astronaut Neil Armstrong became the first humans in history to land and walk on the moon.

as he descended the ladder and, at the last second, hopped onto the powdery surface of the moon. Broadcasting back to Earth, Armstrong said, "That's one small step for man, one giant leap for mankind."[18]

Cuban Missile Crisis

Although winning the space race may have provided the nation with a strong dose of self-esteem, it did little to help settle other Cold War–related fires that were breaking out in the other corners of the globe. In Cuba, a Communist regime under Fidel Castro seized power on January 1, 1959, ousting the American-backed dictator Fulgencio Batista y Zaldívar. American leaders feared that Cuba would fall under the domination of the Soviet Union, meaning the Soviets would establish a presence less than 100 miles (161km) from the American shoreline. When Kennedy entered office he learned the Central Intelligence Agency (CIA) had been making plans to oust Castro in an invasion staged by Cuban exiles. Kennedy gave his approval to continue the plan, and in April 1961 the so-called Bay of Pigs invasion was launched. The invasion would turn out to be a failure, though, as the rebels were quickly captured by Castro's army.

In fact, the Bay of Pigs fiasco drove Castro further into the clutches of the Soviets. In October 1962 US spy planes flying over Cuba photographed the construction of missile launch pads on the island. The implications of the photographs were clear: The Soviets planned to base nuclear weapons in Cuba, within easy striking distance of American cities. Kennedy demanded that the Soviet premier, Nikita Khrushchev, close down the installations and remove whatever missiles were already on the island. He also dispatched US Navy warships to the Caribbean, forming a blockade around Cuba intended to turn back shipments of additional missiles. At first Khrushchev refused, and for thirteen days the United States and Soviet Union stood on the brink of

Operation Pedro Pan

The 2010 US Census reported the Cuban American population at about 1.8 million. Some of those Cubans arrived in America between December 1960 and October 1962 in a mission known as Operation Pedro Pan.

The mission, which was organized by several American charities, was intended to fly Cuban children out of the country so they could escape the Communist regime of Fidel Castro. During the two years of the program, 14,048 children were flown out by airliners chartered by the organizers and then housed in American foster homes. One of those children was Yvonne Conde, who left Cuba at the age of ten. Later she wrote, "Looking back I see that my family really didn't know how long we were going to be separated or what would be my final destination. . . . I left Cuba on August 11, 1961. At that point two hundred unaccompanied Cuban children were arriving in Miami every week." Conde was eventually reunited with her parents, and, after a brief stay in Miami, the Condes moved to Puerto Rico, where they joined a large community of Cuban expatriates.

Yvonne M. Conde, *Operation Pedro Pan*. New York: Routledge, 1999, p. 39.

nuclear warfare, until Khrushchev finally backed down, removed the missiles, and dismantled the pads.

With the Cuban missile crisis behind him, Kennedy turned to that other Cold War hotspot, Vietnam. By the end of 1961, seven hundred US military advisers were based in Vietnam. Clearly, the Communists had been making inroads and were threatening the Diem regime. In 1962 two South Vietnamese fighter pilots defected to the Communists and used their planes to strafe the presidential palace in Saigon. In January 1963 Communist insurgents defeated the South Vietnamese army at the battle of Ap Bac, just 40 miles (64.4km) from Saigon. With the South Vietnamese army clearly outmatched, Kennedy felt he had no choice but to ramp up military aid. By late 1963 more than fifteen thousand American troops would be serving as military advisers in Vietnam, which was also receiving $500 million a year in aid from the US government.

Assassination

But Kennedy himself would fall victim to the Cold War. On November 22, 1963, while on a visit to Dallas, Texas, Kennedy was shot and killed by a gunman hiding in a warehouse along the route of the president's motorcade. Less than an hour later police captured the assassin, Lee Harvey Oswald, after he killed a Dallas policeman. As investigators looked into the life of Oswald, they discovered that he was a former marine who defected to the Soviet Union, then returned to America with a Russian wife. He also held strong sympathies for the Castro regime in Cuba and attempted to organize a pro-Castro movement in the United States.

At first Oswald denied shooting the president, but he would never get to tell his story in court. Two days after his arrest, as police were leading him out of the Dallas city jail, he was shot by Dallas nightclub owner Jack Ruby. After killing Oswald, Ruby told police he was an ardent admirer of Kennedy. As he took Oswald's killer into custody, Dallas police detective Don Archer told Ruby, "Jack, I think you killed him." Ruby replied, "I intended to shoot him three times."[19] Ruby died in prison on January 3, 1967.

The assassination of Kennedy marked a tragic moment in what was otherwise a vibrant time in American history as Kennedy, the astronauts of the American space program, and other national leaders pursued a policy of American exceptionalism. The notion that a culture based on democracy and individual freedoms could excel and grow may not have been widely accepted in places like Vietnam and Cuba, but the success of the Apollo space program unquestionably proved that the American way of life was indeed exceptional and capable of accomplishing the most daunting of challenges.

Chapter 3

Vietnam

Even before President Kennedy's death, Vietnam was turning into a quagmire. The government of Ngo Dinh Diem had grown corrupt while proving itself incapable of waging war against the Communists. After the ouster of Bao Dai, Diem installed himself as the virtual dictator in South Vietnam. He appointed his brother, Ngo Dinh Nhu, head of the country's secret police, which used strong-arm tactics to root out Communist insurgents. Nhu's agents searched for Communists in Saigon and other cities as well as in the country's rural hamlets. Young men were torn away from their homes and families. In many cases they were tortured and murdered by Nhu's agents.

At the time, most Americans were oblivious to the corruption and heavy hand of the Diem government, but in 1963 events unfolded that would lead to the ouster of the Diem government and an escalation in American involvement in the war. On the morning of June 11 Quang Duc, an elderly Buddhist monk, stepped out of a car at a busy Saigon intersection. Sitting cross-legged in the middle of the street, he was doused with gasoline by another monk and set on fire. Quang resorted to self-immolation to call attention to the abuses of the Diem regime. News photographers captured the image, and the next day photographs of the burning monk appeared on front pages across the globe. Soon other Buddhist monks carried out similar sacrifices.

To American diplomats, it was clear Diem was losing control of the country. Secretly, a group of South Vietnamese generals approached Lucien Conein, a CIA official, and asked for American support in toppling Diem. The plan was communicated to Kennedy, who approved the coup but said Diem should first be given the opportunity to resign. Diem refused.

The Gulf of Tonkin Incident

The coup commenced on November 1, 1963, when South Vietnamese military planes strafed the presidential palace in Saigon. Troops moved in and arrested Diem and Nhu, finding the brothers hiding in a Catholic church. Kennedy had hoped for a bloodless coup, but that would not occur. While in custody Diem and Nhu were both shot at point-blank range.

When news of the deaths of Diem and Nhu leaked out, Saigon erupted in celebrations. Portraits of Diem were torn off walls and burned. Political prisoners were released from jail. In Saigon US ambassador Henry Cabot Lodge sent a telegram to Kennedy. "The prospects," Lodge wrote, "are now for a shorter war."[20]

That would turn out to be a bold and incorrect assumption. In August 1964 three North Vietnamese gunboats patrolling the Gulf of Tonkin were alleged to have fired torpedoes at the US Navy destroyer *Maddox*. Two days later the *Maddox* and another US warship, the *Turner Joy*, reported they were under attack. Lyndon B. Johnson, who by now had replaced the assassinated Kennedy in the White House, saw the confrontations as the means to ramp up American involvement in Vietnam. Pressed by Johnson, on August 7, 1964, Congress passed the Gulf of Tonkin Resolution, granting Johnson authority to use force in Vietnam. By the spring of 1965 a full-fledged war was underway in Vietnam.

American bombers were ordered to destroy targets in North Vietnam, while troops were dispatched to the country not as advisers but as fighters. By the end of the year, nearly two hundred thousand American troops would be in country; in 1968 more than five hundred thousand US troops were fighting in Southeast Asia.

By now most Americans were still firmly behind Johnson and his Vietnam policy. In November 1964 Johnson trounced his opponent, Arizona senator Barry Goldwater, in the presidential election. In August 1965 the Gallup Organization polled Americans on their support for the war and found 61 percent endorsed military action in Vietnam.

Southeast Asia 1954–1975

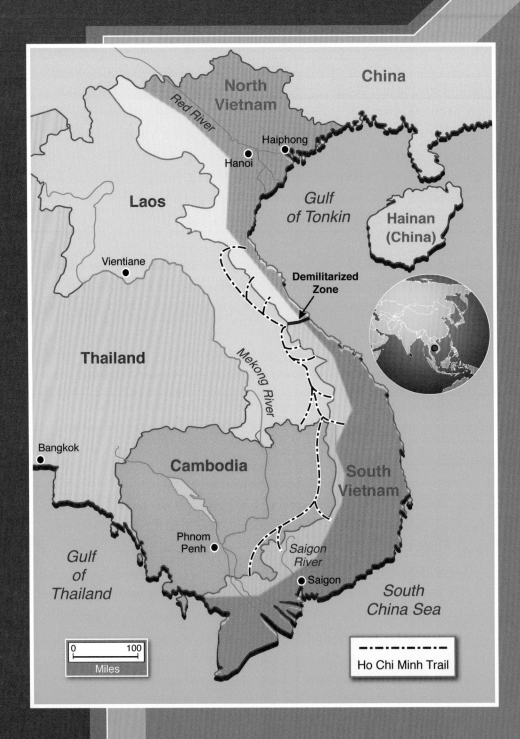

China

North Vietnam

Red River

Haiphong

Hanoi

Laos

Gulf of Tonkin

Hainan (China)

Vientiane

Demilitarized Zone

Thailand

Mekong River

Bangkok

Cambodia

South Vietnam

Phnom Penh

Saigon River

Gulf of Thailand

Saigon

South China Sea

0   100
Miles

Ho Chi Minh Trail

Rolling Thunder

To garner support for the war, Johnson and other national leaders asserted that if Vietnam fell to the Communists the situation would create a domino effect, suggesting the loss of Vietnam would cause other Asian countries to fall under Communist rule. The widely held view that a loss in South Vietnam would embolden the Communists to spread their influence to other countries was stated most clearly several years into the war by defense secretary Robert McNamara. In a March 1967 report to Johnson, McNamara wrote, "Southeast Asia will probably fall under Communist dominance, all of Vietnam, Laos, Cambodia, Burma, Indonesia, Malaysia, Thailand, Philippines, India, Australia, New Zealand, Taiwan, Korea and Japan."[21]

As Johnson and military leaders committed themselves to keeping South Vietnam free from communism, American troops were drawn into fierce warfare. On October 21, 1964, Vietcong guerillas attacked an American air base at Bien Hoa, just some 50 miles (80.5km) north of Saigon, destroying five B-57 bombers and damaging thirteen more planes while killing four Americans and wounding thirty. On February 7, 1965, the Communist guerillas attacked a US Army helicopter base at Pleiku in a mountainous region of the country known as the Central Highlands. Eight Americans were killed and 126 wounded while ten aircraft were destroyed. Four days later the Vietcong struck again, attacking a US Army barracks in the coastal city of Qui Nhon. The attack killed twenty-three Americans.

Meanwhile, for much of the war American planes and ground troops carried on a futile search for what was known as the Ho Chi Minh Trail, a well-hidden pathway from North Vietnam to the south. The trail snaked through neighboring Laos and Cambodia, enabling guerillas to transport arms, ammunition, and other supplies to the Vietcong. "When I frequently scanned the region from helicopters during the 1960s, nothing was discernible, even at low altitudes, beneath the green canopy that seemed to stretch on endlessly," recalls journalist Stanley Karnow. "[The trail] became the route through which North Vietnam [moved] modest shipments of arms, ammunition and other matériel to the Vietcong."[22]

Frustrated by the inability of ground troops to close the munitions supply trails or turn back the guerilla attacks, Johnson ordered Operation Rolling Thunder, a relentless bombing campaign directed at the North. The bombing commenced in March 1965 and lasted through November 1968. During that time, the US Air Force dropped a million tons of bombs on targets in the North. In 1966 alone, the US military staged some seven thousand raids on not only military targets but also roads, vehicles, and bridges—hitting many of the targets more than once. Johnson hoped Rolling Thunder would crack the resolve of the North Vietnamese leaders, but the strategy failed. The North Vietnamese endured the bombings and continued to pursue the war.

The Proxy War

At this point the Vietnam conflict had turned into a proxy war, a conflict in which the main enemies do not engage in direct conflict with one another. In Vietnam, the North Vietnamese and the Vietcong were doing the fighting, but America's true enemies were the Soviet Union and China—the sponsors of international communism. To fight the proxy war in Vietnam, Americans engaged in combat, accompanied by South Vietnamese troops whom they trained and armed. Meanwhile, the North Vietnamese Army as well as the Vietcong received arms and funding from China and the Soviet Union. Those two countries did not supply troops to the conflict; therefore, there was no direct fighting between American troops and the armies of the Soviet Union and China.

As the months of fighting ground on, American leaders insisted US troops maintained an edge. In late 1967 the American military commander in Vietnam, General William Westmoreland, returned to America, giving a rosy picture of American progress. Westmoreland claimed US troops had contained the Vietcong and were in firm control of South Vietnam. "It is not inconceivable that the enemy will realize that he is not in a position where he can win," insisted Westmoreland. "This is what is happening. But apparently the enemy hasn't realized it yet."[23]

When Johnson Lost Cronkite

In 1968 influential TV journalist Walter Cronkite told his audience that he planned to tour Vietnam to see the war for himself. He arrived in Vietnam as the Tet Offensive was underway, witnessing intense fighting in the city of Hue (pronounced hWAY). After returning to New York he told his viewers, "To say we are mired in stalemate seems to be the only realistic, yet unsatisfactory conclusion. It is increasingly clear to this reporter that the only rational way out, then, will be to negotiate, not as victors, but as an honorable people who lived up to their pledge to defend democracy, and did the best they could."

One person who watched Cronkite's broadcast that evening was President Johnson. Following Cronkite's broadcast Johnson turned to an aide and admitted he could no longer count on the American people to support the war. "If I've lost Cronkite," Johnson said, "I've lost middle America."

Walter Cronkite, *A Reporter's Life*. New York: Alfred A. Knopf, 1996, p. 258.

Quoted in Douglas Martin, "Walter Cronkite, 92, Dies; Trusted Voice of TV News," *New York Times*, July 18, 2009, p. 1.

Westmoreland may have been in a boastful mood, but Americans were growing suspicious of his claims of success. By now the war was being fought in full view of the American public. TV correspondents and their camera crews were able to record footage of fierce firefighting, bombings, and other acts of war that were shown nightly on American newscasts as network anchormen reported grim casualty statistics. In November 1966, just two years after the Gulf of Tonkin Resolution, a Gallup poll reported a majority of Americans were now opposed to the war. As Westmoreland visited America and addressed Congress, Gallup reported that 54 percent of Americans opposed the war. As the war continued to drag on, support for it continued to erode. Throughout this period attempts were made to achieve a negotiated peace. In 1968 a peace conference in Paris, France, was established, but diplomats made little progress, and hopes of a negotiated end to the war were regarded as futile.

Evading the Draft

Perhaps no class of individuals was more opposed to the war than the young people of draft age. Their opposition was voiced on college campuses and elsewhere. Among them, such activists as Abbie Hoffman, Jerry Rubin, and Tom Hayden emerged as leaders of demonstrations against the war. Hoffman, Rubin, and others formed a loose coalition known as the Youth International Party, or Yippies, dedicating themselves to protest and stirring up opposition against the war at home.

Draft evasion was common—by the end of the decade, an estimated two hundred thousand American men refused to report for duty. Many were fearful of the intense fighting in the tropical Vietnamese jungles. Others felt a moral and political opposition to the war and believed they had no obligation to protect democracy in a far-off land. One draft resister was Muhammad Ali, the world heavyweight boxing champion. After receiving his military induction notice in 1967, Ali announced he had no intentions of reporting for duty. "I ain't got no quarrel with them Vietcong,"[24] Ali declared. Boxing officials responded by stripping Ali of his title. Ali was later convicted of draft evasion, but his conviction was overturned on appeal.

Some draft resisters fled to Canada to wait out the Vietnam War. Some declared themselves "conscientious objectors," a status that enabled them to serve in noncombat roles. Other draft resisters refused to accept even that role and were willing to face the consequences at home. Many participated in demonstrations where they publicly burned their draft cards. Indeed, during the Vietnam era some nine thousand American men were prosecuted for refusing to report for duty. One was David Harris, the husband of folk singer Joan Baez, who led a draft resistance movement. Harris was charged with evad-

A former Wisconsin college student expresses his opposition to US involvement in the Vietnam War by publicly burning his draft card in 1967. Thousands of young American men refused to report for military service during the war.

ing the draft, convicted, and sentenced to a twenty-month prison term. Years later, he told a reporter why he had evaded the draft and encouraged others to do so as well: "I am certainly not a standard pacifist, but I do believe that there's nothing more serious anybody can do than to kill another human being. . . . And while that may be justified in certain contexts, you've got to have a good reason. And no good reason [in Vietnam] ever materialized."[25]

Political Opposition

Political figures were also voicing opposition to the war. In late 1967 US senator Eugene McCarthy, an ardent opponent of the war, announced he would challenge Johnson in 1968 for the Democratic nomination for president. McCarthy's campaign focused on a single issue: If elected, he would withdraw US troops from Vietnam. McCarthy was given little chance of defeating the incumbent president for the party nomination, but young activists flocked to his campaign and worked hard for McCarthy, concentrating their efforts on New Hampshire—site of the country's first primary. As McCarthy campaigned across New Hampshire, a new wave of fighting erupted in South Vietnam. North Vietnam had launched the Tet Offensive—a massive push into the South launched during Tet, the holiday marking the Vietnamese new year. As election day in New Hampshire neared, the evening news broadcast scenes of intense fighting. Many Americans were horrified by the routine reports of American casualties.

Johnson won the New Hampshire primary—but by a closer margin than anticipated. McCarthy's strong showing revealed a deep division in the Democratic Party over support for the war. Fearing that he would lose the election, Johnson shocked the nation when he announced in late March 1968 that he would withdraw from the race. Just prior to Johnson's exit, Robert F. Kennedy, a New York senator and brother of the former president, had announced his candidacy for the Democratic nomination. Soon after Johnson's exit, Hubert H. Humphrey, the vice president, joined the race as well.

Kennedy's campaign seemed to be gaining the most traction among voters, but after winning the California primary in June 1968 he was assassinated by a Middle Eastern terrorist, Sirhan Sirhan. The killer later told investigators that he opposed Kennedy because of the candidate's support for the nation of Israel.

Trial of the Chicago Seven

Humphrey was now his party's most likely nominee. Fearing that Humphrey would continue Johnson's policies in Vietnam, antiwar activists descended on Chicago in August to demonstrate against the war as party leaders gathered for the Democratic National Convention. For four days chaos reigned both inside the convention hall and on the streets of the city as police—dispatched by the city's no-nonsense mayor Richard

The My Lai Massacre

One of the darkest chapters in the Vietnam War occurred in My Lai, a village in South Vietnam. On March 16, 1968, a US Army unit known as Charlie Company entered the village searching for Vietcong fighters. Instead, they found mostly women, children, and elderly people. Allegedly under orders from Lieutenant William Calley, the soldiers opened fire on the villagers, murdering some three hundred innocent people. The army attempted to cover up the incident, but in 1969 a member of another unit heard about the massacre from members of Charlie Company and contacted journalist Seymour Hersh, whose account of the incident was published in thirty American newspapers.

Calley as well as twelve other officers were put on trial, but only Calley was convicted. He was sentenced to life imprisonment in the stockade at Fort Benning, Georgia. His sentence was later reduced to twenty years, but he was released after spending just three years in detention.

J. Daley—used strong-arm tactics to quell the demonstrations. In their homes, horrified Americans watched as TV cameras recorded the riots and the Chicago police's brutal treatment of the protesters. Eventually, Humphrey was nominated. Meanwhile, eight leaders of the protest were singled out as ringleaders and prosecuted. When the case of black activist Bobby Seale was prosecuted separately, the remaining defendants became known as the Chicago Seven.

The trial of the Chicago Seven—Hoffman, Rubin, and Hayden as well as Rennie Davis, David Dellinger, John Froines, and Lee Weiner—commenced in March 1969. The defendants treated the proceedings with contempt. They battled often with Judge Julius Hoffman (no relation to Abbie Hoffman), whom they accused of favoring the prosecution. "We wanted to reach young people," Abbie Hoffman said. "We wanted to show we were different from those prosecuting us. We wanted to present a synopsis of the issues dividing the nation, thereby elevating our cause to equal footing with the government."[26]

The trial lasted five months, earning widespread coverage in the media and exposing the deep divisions among the American people over the war. When the verdicts were read, Davis, Dellinger, Hayden, Hoffman, and Rubin were convicted of a single charge of inciting a riot but acquitted of conspiracy charges. Froines and Weiner were acquitted of all charges. Three years later an appeals court overturned all convictions, finding that Judge Hoffman had been biased.

As for Seale, during his trial his frequent outbursts prompted the judge to have him bound and gagged in the courtroom. Because of his outbursts he was convicted of contempt of court and sentenced to four years in prison.

The Woodstock Generation

While the Democratic Party was at war with itself over Vietnam, the Republican Party was experiencing far less dissent in its ranks. Richard Nixon, making a political comeback following his defeat by Kennedy eight years earlier, quickly sewed up the nomination. Nixon portrayed himself as a figure of stability and appealed to the "silent majority" of Americans—those who were not taking to the streets but were demanding law and order—to support him. Nixon also assured Americans he had a plan to end the war but refused to provide details. Putting their trust in the Republican, Americans elected Nixon by a slim margin over Humphrey and an independent candidate, Alabama governor George Wallace.

As it turned out, many young Americans would be sorely disappointed with Nixon's plan to end the war. Instead of a quick withdrawal, Nixon initiated a relentless bombing of the North. Still, by the end of 1969 the war seemed as though it would have no end. The Vietcong continued its guerilla campaign in the South as American troops failed to cut off their supplies over the Ho Chi Minh Trail. Meanwhile, dissent and protest remained very much a part of American life. In August 1969 an estimated half-million young people converged on a farm near the small upstate New York town of Woodstock, where organizers staged a rock concert.

Woodstock turned into much more than a concert. Instead, it became a rallying center for opposition to the war. Many of the performers played antiwar songs and gave speeches condemning the war. Perhaps one of the most popular songs to emerge from Woodstock was "I Feel Like I'm Fixin' to Die Rag" by the band Country Joe and the Fish, which told of a young draftee on his way to Vietnam and his sincere belief that he would die there. One Woodstock attendee was Abbie Hoffman, awaiting his sentencing following the Chicago Seven verdict. He called Woodstock, "A musical festival. An event. A city. And finally a symbol of hope. New Nation had a name, and for years we would be known as the 'Woodstock Generation.'"[27]

Chapter 4

The Fight for Social Justice

On February 1, 1960, four young African American students at North Carolina A&T College walked into the Woolworth department Store in Greensboro, North Carolina. They sat down at the lunch counter, waiting to be served. For the four young men, it was a bold and brave action. In 1960 the Jim Crow laws found in the southern states strictly prohibited blacks from being served together with whites. If restaurants did serve both races, it was typical for them to feature separate blacks-only entrances and small dining areas, usually in their kitchens.

The Jim Crow laws had been on the books in the South for decades, some dating back to the years after Reconstruction when state legislatures as well as city governments concocted measures to segregate schools, theaters, restaurants, and other public places. (Jim Crow was a character in the old minstrel shows of the nineteenth century, typically played by white actors wearing blackface makeup, portraying African Americans as happy-go-lucky yet subservient.)

The "Greensboro Four"—Joseph McNeil, Ezell Blair Jr., David Richmond, and Franklin McCain—were well aware of the Jim Crow laws in North Carolina and knew they would be refused service. Yet they aimed to protest the discriminatory laws of their state. "My parents grew up and carried the scars of racial segregation," says McNeil, who went on to a career in the US Air Force, rising to the rank of general. "I didn't want to see my children have to face the same problem. We just felt that this certainly was a time to act. If not now, when? If not my generation, what generation?"[28]

Separate but Unequal

As expected, they were refused service. Still, the Greensboro Four sat at the counter for hours before finally leaving and moving on to another department store lunch counter. Over the next two weeks, they staged sit-ins at five department store lunch counters in Greensboro. Soon, other black students staged sit-ins at lunch counters throughout the city. By the end of the month, the police had declared a crackdown and started to arrest the demonstrators—more than eighty were taken into custody as they sat peacefully at lunch counters in whites-only establishments. Meanwhile, the movement spread to other cities. Within a few months, thousands of black college students staged sit-ins at whites-only lunch counters throughout the South.

The civil rights movement had started the decade before with the Rosa Parks incident, the Montgomery bus boycott, and the 1954 *Brown v. Board of Education* decision by the US Supreme Court. In that case an African American parent, Oliver Brown, and several other parents sued the Board of Education of Topeka, Kansas, asserting that segregated schools were unconstitutional.

The Supreme Court's decision in the *Brown* case overturned an 1896 Supreme Court decision known as *Plessy v. Ferguson*. In that case the court ruled that a "separate but equal" society was legal under the US Constitution. This ruling meant that the races could be separated in schools and other institutions as long as they received equal access to education, transportation, and other facets of life.

But life in the southern states—and in some places in the northern states too—was never equal. Schools for African Americans typically lacked an adequate number of books and other educational supplies. There were also fewer schools for blacks, meaning black students often had to walk long distances to attend classes. Oliver Brown's seven-year-old daughter Linda had to walk a mile each day, crossing through a dangerous railroad switchyard, to attend her elementary school. As for transportation, blacks may have been permitted to ride on the same trains as whites, but they were invariably crowded into one or two cars in the back of the train, forced to ride long distances crammed together in tight quarters. In the other cars, whites enjoyed far more comfortable conditions. And, as the Parks incident illustrated, when a white passenger boarded a bus and found no seat available, under the Jim Crow laws a black passenger was forced to give up his or her seat.

The Freedom Rides

In 1961 activists for the civil rights group Congress of Racial Equality (CORE) aimed to desegregate public transportation. By now they had the law on their side. In 1946 a Supreme Court decision had ruled the segregation of interstate transportation unconstitutional. And in 1955 the US Interstate Commerce Commission, an agency of the federal government, declared segregated transportation violated the US Interstate Commerce Act.

Still, segregated buses and trains were very much a part of life in the South as the states clung to their Jim Crow laws. On May 4, 1961, thirteen CORE activists, including blacks and whites, boarded two buses in Washington, DC, aiming to keep their seats as the buses made their way through Georgia, Alabama, South Carolina, and Mississippi. John Lewis, an African American from South Carolina who would later be elected to Congress, rode aboard one of the buses. He sat alongside Arthur Bigelow, a white man from Connecticut. "When we got to South Carolina, the bus arrived in a little town called Rock Hill," Lewis recalls. "Arthur and I, walking together, tried to enter the white waiting room. Several young white men met us at the door, and when we tried to open it, they knocked us down in the street and began beating us with their fists. We both shed a little blood."[29]

More trouble arrived in Anniston, Alabama, where the two buses were met by racist whites who set one of the vehicles on fire. The riders on that bus as well as the other vehicle were pulled off and beaten.

The incident touched off a movement known as the Freedom Rides, in which thousands of other activists took similar bus trips, refusing to give up their seats to whites or otherwise abide by Jim Crow segregation. And their ranks included not just African Americans but whites as well. Young people, particularly college students, were inspired by the crusade and joined the black riders, making Freedom Rides alongside them.

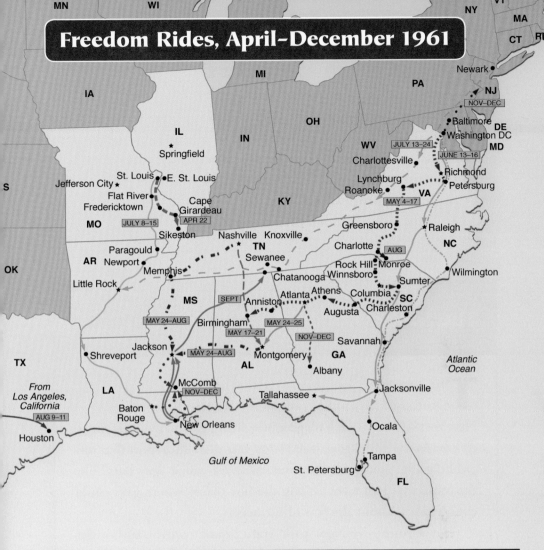

Freedom Rides, April–December 1961

MN · WI · VT · NH · NY · MA · CT · RI · MI · PA · IA · OH · IN · IL · Springfield · KY · WV · Charlottesville · Lynchburg · Roanoke · Richmond · Petersburg · VA · Baltimore · Washington DC · DE · MD · JULY 13–24 · JUNE 13–16 · MAY 4–17 · St. Louis · E. St. Louis · Jefferson City · Flat River · Fredericktown · Cape Girardeau · JULY 8–15 · APR 22 · MO · Sikeston · Paragould · Newport · AR · Memphis · Little Rock · Nashville · Knoxville · TN · Sewanee · Chatanooga · MS · SEPT · Anniston · Atlanta · Athens · Birmingham · MAY 24–AUG · MAY 17–21 · MAY 24–25 · NOV–DEC · Jackson · MAY 24–AUG · Shreveport · Montgomery · AL · McComb · NOV–DEC · LA · Baton Rouge · New Orleans · Houston · From Los Angeles, California · AUG 9–11 · TX · Greensboro · Raleigh · NC · Charlotte · AUG · Rock Hill · Monroe · Winnsboro · Sumter · Wilmington · Columbia · SC · Augusta · Charleston · Savannah · GA · Albany · Tallahassee · Jacksonville · Ocala · Tampa · St. Petersburg · FL · Atlantic Ocean · Gulf of Mexico · Newark · NJ · OK · S · Little Rock

- Little Freedom Ride, April 22
- Original CORE Freedom Ride, May 4–17
- Nashville Movement Freedom Ride, May 17–21
- Mississippi Freedom Rides, May 24–August
- Connecticut Freedom Ride, May 24–25
- Interfaith Freedom Ride, June 13–16
- Organized Labor/Professional Freedom Ride, June 13–16
- Missouri to Louisiana CORE Freedom Ride, July 8–15
- New Jersey to Arkansas CORE Freedom Ride, July 13–24
- Los Angeles to Houston Freedom Ride, August 9–11
- Monroe Freedom Ride, August
- Prayer Pilgrimage Freedom Ride, September
- Albany Freedom Rides, November–December
- McComb Freedom Rides, November–December
- Route 40 Campaign, November–December

The Free Speech Movement

The presence of whites alongside blacks on the Freedom Rides illustrated growing sympathy for the African American cause. In no place was this truer than on college campuses, where many students supported racial equality and called for school administrators to provide more opportunities for black students. But the campus crusaders often met with hostility from school administrators, who opposed not only activism for racial equality on their campuses but activism for any political cause whatsoever.

The Stonewall Riot

The campaign for gay rights can be traced to the 1960s, prompted by a police raid on the Stonewall Inn, a tavern in New York's Greenwich Village where many gay people met to socialize. At the time, gays faced such vast discrimination that few publicly admitted their homosexuality. So-called "gay bars" like the Stonewall Inn were among the few places where gays could congregate without the fear of ostracism.

But a ruling by New York State liquor control authorities banned homosexuals in groups larger than three from congregating in bars. On June 27, 1969, police raided the Stonewall Inn. In making arrests, police struggled with the patrons inside in a melee that left three officers injured. As word of the raid spread through the New York gay community, hundreds of gay men and women flocked to the neighborhood and rioted. The riot galvanized the gay community into action, and soon activists formed the Gay Liberation Front to work for gay rights. On the first anniversary of the riot, ten thousand gays and their supporters staged a march in support of gay rights. That march led to the establishment of Gay Pride Weeks in New York and other cities.

At the University of California at Berkeley, students resolved to challenge the policy. On October 1, 1964, Berkeley student Jack Weinberg was arrested by campus police for passing out literature published by CORE. At the time, the Berkeley administration had banned all political activity on campus, angering some students who made Freedom Rides and wanted to draft other students for the civil rights cause. When Weinberg was arrested and placed into a campus police car, the vehicle was quickly surrounded by hundreds of students who demanded his release and refused to move.

Weinberg was eventually released, but a movement had been born. Soon the campaign became known as the free speech movement, which spawned months of demonstrations on the Berkeley campus. The Berkeley demonstrations proved to be an important chapter in the campaign for free speech because it helped draw the young people of the 1960s—the baby boomers—into the national campaign for social justice. In the weeks following Weinberg's arrest, other demonstrations followed, including a massive sit-in staged in the university's Sproul Hall on December 1, 1964, in which more than a thousand students participated. They demanded the right to organize political activities on campus, stage protests, give speeches, and set up tables to distribute pamphlets and other literature trumpeting political and social causes. After months of similar demonstrations, the university finally relented and permitted students to use the campus to organize political movements and stage protests.

James Meredith and the University of Mississippi

One university that stood steadfast against political activism—particularly civil rights activism—was the University of Mississippi. The antisegregation war being waged at bus stops and train stations throughout the South had also come to universities, with black students fighting to gain admission to whites-only colleges. In 1962 black student James Meredith won a federal court order permitting him to enroll in the University of Mississippi. On September 20 Meredith arrived at the campus in the city of Oxford. He was met by Mississippi governor Ross Barnett, who personally blocked Meredith's entrance and turned him away.

President Kennedy took dramatic steps to force the university to admit Meredith. Kennedy dispatched five hundred federal marshals to accompany Meredith to the university to ensure he would be permitted to enroll. As Meredith and the marshals headed for the university, hundreds of supporters of segregation staged a rally in Oxford, vowing to confront the marshals. As the attendees waved hundreds of Confederate flags, Barnett declared, "I love our people, I love our ways, I love our traditions."[30]

The confrontation at the university occurred on October 1, 1962. It soon turned violent as members of the angry crowd shot at the marshals, wounding twenty-six. Two bystanders were killed by stray fire. Kennedy sent five thousand US troops to the scene to support the marshals, and at that point the troops moved in to quell the violence. Meredith was finally admitted to the university; he graduated in 1964.

"I Have a Dream"

Although the Freedom Rides, free speech movement, and Meredith case garnered headlines and dominated the network newscasts, the watershed event in the campaign for civil rights occurred on August 28, 1963, when some two hundred thousand supporters of civil rights marched on Washington, DC. There they heard Martin Luther King Jr. deliver his "I Have a Dream" speech, calling for Americans to recognize the equality of the races. Standing on the steps of the Lincoln Memorial, King faced the huge crowd gathered before him on the National Mall and declared:

> I say to you today, my friends, so even though we face the difficulties of today and tomorrow, I still have a dream. It is a dream deeply rooted in the American dream.
>
> I have a dream that one day this nation will rise up and live out the true meaning of its creed: "We hold these truths to be self-evident: that all men are created equal."
>
> I have a dream that one day on the red hills of Georgia the sons of former slaves and the sons of former slave owners will be able to sit down together at the table of brotherhood.

I have a dream that one day even the state of Mississippi, a state sweltering with the heat of injustice, sweltering with the heat of oppression, will be transformed into an oasis of freedom and justice.

I have a dream that my four little children will one day live in a nation where they will not be judged by the color of their skin but by the content of their character.[31]

Landmark Legislation

Given the overwhelming evidence that many African Americans were still burdened by Jim Crow laws and facing inequality, new civil rights legislation was clearly needed. In 1964 President Johnson signed the landmark Civil Rights Act. The law made it illegal to maintain discriminatory practices in all public places—schools, theaters, and bus stations, among them. Under the act, to bar people from public places on the basis of race, gender, or national origin is a federal crime.

Moreover, the act empowered the federal government to cut off financial aid to any state or city found to be in violation of the law. Each year the federal government makes billions of dollars available to state and municipal governments to help them build and repair streets, bridges, and other infrastructure such as water filtration and sewage treatment plants. Federal funds are also doled out to help run schools, social services programs, and assist local communities in maintaining police forces. Dozens of other local services would also be impossible to maintain without access to federal subsidies. By keeping their Jim Crow laws on the books, state governments and local communities risked losing that funding.

Violent Reactions

Some Americans regarded the changes mandated by the Civil Rights Act as too radical; they were not prepared to accept African Americans and other minority members as equals. The early 1960s marked the rebirth of the Ku Klux Klan. When founded in the years following the

Civil War, hooded Klansmen terrorized blacks through kidnappings and lynchings. By 1925 the Klan enjoyed a rebirth, staging a public march on Washington in which some fifty thousand hooded Klansmen participated. By the 1960s the Klan had reverted to its terrorist traditions, bombing black churches and schools and finding other ways to commit violence against African Americans.

In 1964 three civil rights workers—Michael Schwerner and Andrew Goodman, who were white, and James Chaney, an African American—were murdered near the small town of Philadelphia, Mississippi. State authorities refused to investigate the crime, but a probe by the Federal Bureau of Investigation found that several Klansmen conspired to kill the victims. Eighteen defendants were charged with the murders in federal court, but convictions were won against just six. None of the defendants received prison sentences longer than ten years. However, the investigation continued. In 2005, a Klan ringleader, Edgar Ray Killen, was convicted in the murders and sentenced to sixty years in prison.

Possibly the most shocking response to the civil rights movement of the 1960s was the assassination of King. On April 3, 1968, the civil rights leader arrived in Memphis, Tennessee, to lend his support to a strike staged by black sanitation workers. The following day, as King and his aides stood on the balcony of the Lorraine Motel in downtown Memphis, a shot struck King in the face. Rushed to a local hospital, King was declared dead within hours.

Witnesses reported that King had been shot from the window of a nearby boarding house, and moments after the shot was fired a man ran from the boarding house carrying a bundle. He was identified as James Earl Ray, a small-time thief and fugitive who escaped the year before from a Missouri prison. Police finally caught up with Ray at Heathrow Airport in London, England. He confessed to the murder and was sentenced to ninety-nine years in prison. Ray died in prison in 1998.

Feminists Raise Their Voices

The civil rights movement did not end with the murder of King or the deaths of other activists such as Medgar Evers, an official of the Na-

Robed Ku Klux Klan members gather in 1964 in Atlanta, Georgia. The 1960s saw a resurgence of Klan activity, a response to civil rights laws that promised equal treatment for African Americans and other disenfranchised groups.

tional Association for the Advancement of Colored People (NAACP), who was murdered in 1963. (It took until 1994 to identify and convict Evers's killer, Ku Klux Klan member Byron De La Beckwith, who died in prison in 2001.) The work by these civil rights activists helped make it illegal to discriminate against blacks, but others benefited from the 1964 Civil Rights Act as well.

Women were often denied job opportunities and equal pay with men. In 1963 the feminist movement found its voice in author Betty Friedan, whose bestselling book *The Feminine Mystique* found that many women felt American society confined them to roles as housewives and mothers. Many wished to lead professional lives. Describing the plight of women in 1960s America, Friedan writes,

> The problem lay buried, unspoken, for many years in the minds of American women. It was a strange stirring, a sense of dissatisfaction, a yearning that women suffered in the middle of the twentieth century in the United States. Each suburban wife struggled with it alone. As she made the beds, shopped for groceries, matched slipcover material, ate peanut butter sandwiches with her children, chauffeured Cub Scouts and Brownies, lay beside her husband at night—she was afraid to ask even of herself the silent question—"Is this all?"[32]

The issue of unfairness to women had actually reached the White House two years before Friedan published her book, when Kennedy appointed the President's Commission on the Status of Women. The commission reported that women suffered widespread discrimination in the workplace, particularly in the salaries they earned: Many women were paid less than their male counterparts even though they held similar jobs.

In 1963 Congress responded by passing the Equal Pay Act, which made it illegal to pay women lower salaries for the same jobs held by men. The Civil Rights Act of 1964 added new strength to the movement—as with discrimination in theaters and bus stations, the law made discrimination in the workplace illegal as well.

Birth of the Environmental Movement

While Friedan's book helped spawn feminism, another book published during the early 1960s helped launch the environmental movement in America. In 1962 Rachel Carson published *Silent Spring* in which the author targeted the use of pesticides in agricultural production, primarily dichlorodiphenyltrichloroethane (DDT). Carson's book would lead to a ban on the pesticide in 1972. Congress responded to other environmental concerns, adopting the first Clean Air Act in 1963. Stronger

Loving vs. Virginia

By the 1960s it was still illegal in nineteen states for couples of different races to marry. These "antimiscegenation" laws were overturned by the US Supreme Court in a case brought by Richard and Mildred Loving. Richard, a white man, married Mildred, a black woman, in 1958. Residents of Virginia, the Lovings drove eighty miles north to Washington, DC, to be married because of their state's law banning interracial marriage. After returning to Virginia, they were arrested for breaking a law that had been on the books in Virginia since 1691—when the state was still an English colony.

The Lovings were sentenced to a year in prison, but the judge said he would suspend the sentence if the Lovings agreed to leave Virginia. The couple accepted the offer and moved to Washington, but they also challenged the law. On June 12, 1967, the Supreme Court ruled unanimously that antimiscegenation laws were unconstitutional. Wrote Chief Justice Earl Warren, "Marriage is one of the 'basic civil rights of man,' fundamental to our very existence and survival. To deny this fundamental freedom . . . is surely to deprive all the state's citizens of liberty."

Quoted in University of Missouri–Kansas City School of Law, "*Loving vs. Virginia*," 2012. http://law2.umkc.edu.

environmental legislation, such as the Clean Water Act and amendments that would toughen the Clean Air Act, would not be passed until the 1970s and 1980s.

Nevertheless, Carson is given credit for opening the eyes of Americans not only to the hazards of chemical pesticides but also to the dangers to the environment caused by the discharge of industrial waste into rivers and streams as well as the poisonous fumes released into the air by automobiles and factories. "Carson's thesis that we were subjecting ourselves to slow poisoning by misuse of chemical pesticides that polluted the environment may seem like common currency now, but in 1962 *Silent Spring* contained the kernel of social revolution,"[33] says environmentalist Linda Lear.

Positive Change

The efforts by such activists as the Greensboro Four as well as King, Friedan, and Carson illustrate that while the American government and people may have spent much of the decade debating the merits of a war fought in a far-off Asian country, many issues at home demanded attention as well. And although the war at home over social justice was often ugly and violent, it did produce positive change that would affect the lives of all Americans.

Chapter 5

Birth of a New American Culture

For much of the 1950s and 1960s, Ed Sullivan was one of the most popular personalities on TV. Each Sunday at 8 p.m. the former newspaper gossip columnist hosted a TV variety show, *The Ed Sullivan Show*, that was watched by millions. Typically, his guests included singers, dancers, and comedians. In 1956 Elvis Presley appeared on Sullivan's show, delivering blockbuster ratings.

In late 1963 Sullivan and his wife Sylvia stepped off an airplane at London's Heathrow Airport, unexpectedly finding themselves in a sea of thousands of teenagers who had been waiting for hours in the rain. When Sullivan asked what all the commotion was about, he was told the teenagers were awaiting the arrival of the rock 'n' roll band the Beatles, due home that day from a tour of Sweden. At that point, Sullivan knew very little about the Beatles—but he knew he wanted them for his show.

For years the Beatles—John Lennon, Paul McCartney, George Harrison, and Ringo Starr—had been enjoying modest success, playing small clubs in Hamburg, Germany, and other European cities. But in 1963 the Beatles released their first album, *Please Please Me*, catapulting the group to overnight stardom in Great Britain and the rest of Europe. Because the Beatles were still mostly unknown in America, their manager, Brian Epstein, was delighted when a New York TV producer called and offered to book the "Fab Four" on *The Ed Sullivan Show* early in 1964.

A Mark of Rebellion

Epstein arranged for the Beatles to make three consecutive appearances on Sullivan's show in February 1964. Almost immediately, hype surrounding the debut started building. The CBS television network—which aired Sullivan's show—received fifty thousand requests for seats. Two days before the show, when the Beatles' plane arrived in New York, three thousand teenage fans were waiting for them. Finally, at 8 p.m. on February 9, some 73 million Americans tuned in to *The Ed Sullivan Show*. After walking onto the stage, Sullivan told his audience, "This city never has witnessed the excitement stirred by these youngsters from Liverpool who call themselves the Beatles. Now tonight, you're gonna twice be entertained by them. . . . Ladies and gentlemen, the Beatles! Let's bring them on."[34]

During their appearances on the Sullivan show, the Beatles wore conservative dark suits, white shirts, and thin ties—but they each also wore a mop of floppy long hair that was not yet in style in America where teenage boys usually sported crew cuts. That would soon change. Much to their parents' displeasure, many of their teenage sons started letting their hair grow.

Long hair was an early mark of rebellion among the teenagers of the early 1960s. Certainly, rock 'n' roll was well established in America by the time the Beatles appeared on the Sullivan show, but the most popular performers included Presley and Frankie Avalon, Fabian Forte, and Bobby Rydell: clean-cut heartthrobs who recorded romantic ballads while pursuing movie careers. Starting in 1963, Avalon and Annette Funicello—a former cast member of *The Mickey Mouse Club*—were stars of the enormously popular series of *Beach Party* movies. These films typically featured paper-thin plots but served as showcases for the singing talents of the stars as well as the shapely figures of the bikini-clad dancers.

The Beatles were joined on American soil by other groups from Great Britain as part of what became known as the British Invasion. Soon, the Rolling Stones, featuring Mick Jagger, as well as the Kinks, the Who, the Dave Clark Five, and the Animals were releasing hits

The Beatles, "Helter Skelter," and Charles Manson

The Beatles often sang about peace and love but one of their songs, "Helter Skelter," sparked one of the most tragic events of the 1960s. Charles Manson, a small-time criminal, lived on a commune in the California desert where his followers revered him. When the Beatles released the song "Helter Skelter" in 1968, Manson believed it foretold the end of the world. "Are you hep to what the Beatles are saying?" Manson told his followers. "Helter Skelter is coming down. The Beatles are telling it like it is."

Manson believed a race war pitting whites against blacks was imminent. To spark the war, he ordered his followers to commit a series of grisly murders, hoping whites would accuse blacks of the crimes, launching the war. As for Manson, he would hide in the desert, wait out the race war, and emerge as leader of a new society. The murders occurred on the nights of August 8 and 9, 1969. In all, seven people were viciously murdered, including movie actress Sharon Tate, who was pregnant at the time, and coffee heiress Abigail Folger. Police eventually cracked the case. Manson and four followers were convicted. By 2012 all were still inmates in California prisons.

Vincent Bugliosi and Curt Gentry, *Helter Skelter: The True Story of the Manson Murders*. New York: W.W. Norton, 1994, p. 327.

to American fans. Some of these groups brought a harder edge to the music than fans were used to hearing from the Beatles. Indeed, many of these bands, as well as home-grown rock acts such as Jimi Hendrix, Janis Joplin, the Doors, Bob Dylan, and Jefferson Airplane, were recording songs about drug use and free love.

Free Love and Hippies

To the young people of the 1960s, free love meant promiscuous sex. For years, teenage girls had been admonished by their parents and sex education teachers to abstain from sexual activity, and teenage boys had been taught to respect their girlfriends. But these messages started falling on deaf ears in the 1960s, thanks largely to the widespread availability of the birth control pill. Under development by pharmaceutical companies for decades, "the pill," as it was commonly known, was approved by the US Food and Drug Administration as an oral contraceptive for women in 1960. By 1965, 6.5 million American women—many of them young and unmarried—were using the pill. With access to birth control, many young women felt empowered to defy the conservative conventions of the past and sleep with whomever they desired.

The availability of the pill and the change in attitude among women toward pre-marital sex helped bring about the era of free love. Young and unmarried men and women lived with one another and, sometimes, lived with several other couples in what were known as communes. In commune life, sharing sexual partners was not unusual.

This new attitude toward sex as well as the overall rebellious nature against many conservative conventions of American society were all part of what was known as "hippie" culture, a term that was first used by *San Francisco Chronicle* reporter Michael Fallon in a 1965 story he wrote about the Blue Unicorn coffeehouse. The Blue Unicorn was a favorite hippie hangout in the city's Haight-Ashbury district. Fallon found that the hippies had virtually dropped out of American society, living in a culture they created for themselves. Men grew their hair long. Hippie men and women dressed casually in blue jeans and T-shirts; few held jobs. They opposed the war in Vietnam. "Hippies considered mainstream society false," says Neil A. Hamilton, historian at Spring Hill College in Alabama. "They rejected its pre-occupation with material goods, its manipulations, its vacuous politics; they rejected its

Guitars and peace symbols punctuate a hippie gathering in San Francisco's Haight-Ashbury district in 1967. Hippie culture took root here and in other cities around the country during the 1960s.

eight-to-five job routine, its conformist suburbs, its impersonal technology. . . . They believed not in the goodness of all but in the value of all human beings, and that people should do what they want as long as they did not hurt others."[35]

Haight-Ashbury was ground zero in what had become known as the "counterculture," but hippies and commune life could be found in many American cities. Hippies gravitated to Greenwich Village in New York City as well as neighborhoods in other cities. Many communes could be found in rural communities where members grew their own food. In 1967, when *Boston Globe* reporter Robert L. Levey visited a commune in the city's Fort Hill neighborhood, he wrote, "They have forsaken most of the middle-class values to which the average person is bound. Few

The Hell's Angels

An element of the counterculture that many Americans found hard to accept were the outlaw motorcycle gangs that formed during the 1960s. The gang members often lived vagabond lives, traveling on their cycles whenever possessed by the mood to move on. But most were also thugs with few scruples, always ready to settle an argument with their fists.

The most familiar of these gangs was the Hell's Angels, which was chronicled in the 1966 book *Hell's Angels: A Strange and Terrible Saga* by journalist Hunter S. Thompson. Quoting one member of the Angels in his book, Thompson writes, "We're the one percenters man—the one percent who don't fit and don't care. . . . We've punched our way out of a hundred rumbles, stayed alive with our boots and our fists. We're royalty among motorcycle outlaws, baby."

Quoted in Hunter S. Thompson, *Hell's Angels: A Strange and Terrible Saga*. New York: Random House, 1966, p. 5.

of them are formally married. They dress with indifferent informality or eccentric care. They spend long nights talking in groups—criticizing each other, probing in vivid detail each other's thoughts."[36]

The Drug Culture

Use of drugs was a big part of the counterculture and certainly appeared in other corners of American life as well. Most drug-using young people favored marijuana, which could provide a peaceful, euphoric feeling in its users, but harsher drugs were also widely consumed. During the 1960s many people discovered the so-called psychedelic effects of lysergic acid diethylamide, more popularly known as LSD or acid. LSD was considered a mind-altering drug, able to create a dream world of hallucinatory images and sounds. Taking LSD was known as "tripping," because an LSD trip could transport the user into a surreal, mind-bending universe where people and places took on supernatural dimensions.

LSD's most prominent and vocal proponent was a former Harvard University professor, Timothy Leary, who experimented with the drug and advocated its use. Leary resigned from the Harvard faculty in 1963 after giving drugs to students, which appalled university officials who were preparing to fire him. Throughout the 1960s, Leary traveled the world learning what he could about LSD, using the drug and advocating its use by others. He lived off the benevolence of friends and fees he collected as a lecturer.

Another LSD advocate during the 1960s was the novelist Ken Kesey. In 1964 Kesey published the novel *Sometimes a Great Notion*. The novel's publisher planned to release the book at the New York World's Fair. Living in the California community of La Honda near San Francisco at the time, Kesey decided to make the trip to New York by way of a cross-country bus ride. He purchased an old school bus, had it painted in psychedelic colors and wired for sound. Kesey and a group of friends dubbed themselves the "Merry Pranksters" and traveled cross-country, stopping often to mingle with local hippies and "dropping" copious amounts of acid along the way.

Flower Power

Drug use was often reflected in the music of the era. Among the hits of the 1960s were "White Rabbit" by Jefferson Airplane and "Purple Haze" by Hendrix, both of which tell stories of drug consumption. Many of these stars were also heavy abusers of drugs. Among the rock stars of the 1960s who died of drug overdoses were Hendrix, Joplin, and Jim Morrison, lead singer for the Doors. Even the Beatles were known to drop references about drugs into their songs. Critics could not help but notice that the key words in the title of the band's 1967 hit "Lucy in the Sky with Diamonds" starts with the letters L, S, and D or that a Beatles song from the same year, "Strawberry Fields Forever," includes lyrics that could be interpreted as describing an LSD experience.

But music did not have to be about drugs to reflect the rebellious attitude of the 1960s. In 1967 the band Steppenwolf released a major hit, "Born to Be Wild," which reflects the generation's desire to break away and leave behind all responsibility.

Meanwhile, the music of the era started reflecting the changing political climate of the 1960s. When the Beatles debuted on *The Ed Sullivan Show*, they performed songs of romance. As the decade moved on, their songs took on a decidedly political—and antiwar—slant. By the end of the decade the repertoire of the Beatles featured a heavy dose of antiwar messages in such songs as "Revolution" and "Let It Be," while Lennon recorded "Give Peace a Chance" on his own. Such stars as Dylan, Melanie, Arlo Guthrie, the Byrds, Donovan, and Crosby, Stills, Nash & Young were all major voices in the 1960s protest movement.

The phrase "flower power" became common in the era—its adherents believed that nonviolence was preferable to waging war in Southeast Asia. One of the most familiar photographs of the era features a young woman, Jan Rose Kamir, placing a flower into the barrel of a rifle wielded by a soldier who had been called out to keep the peace at a 1967 antiwar rally at the Pentagon, headquarters of the US military. Another familiar phrase of the era was "Make love, not war." The slogan is believed to have been first printed on buttons and distributed for free in 1967 at a Chicago bookstore owned by radical activists Franklin and Penelope Rosemont.

Sharing Tea with Goldie

Music was not the only artistic medium to reflect change and rebellion. Landmark books of the era included Harper Lee's *To Kill a Mockingbird*, which weaves a tale around the vicious racism of the South; Philip Roth's *Portnoy's Complaint*, a story of a young man's sexual awakening; and Joseph Heller's *Catch-22*, a novel about World War II that carries a clear antiwar and antiauthority message.

Another important book discovered by Americans in the 1960s was Henry Miller's novel *Tropic of Cancer*, which was first published in France in 1934 but banned from import by the US Customs Service because the agency considered the prose too sexually explicit for American readers. In 1961 New York publisher Grove Press defied American censorship laws and published the novel for American readers, touching off a landmark free speech case. When the American edition was published, government officials in several states filed lawsuits against Grove, prohibiting sales of the book in their states. In 1964 the case was decided by the US Supreme Court, which found that governments have extremely limited authority to ban the work of writers and other creative people, particularly on the basis of what the government may regard as obscene. The ruling permitted the sale of *Tropic of Cancer* to American readers and opened the way for other creative people to test the tolerance of the public for content that for years had been regarded as taboo.

Television was one medium where creative people pushed the limits of what had been regarded as acceptable programming. During the early years of the decade, TV viewers could tune in to such family-friendly fare as *Gunsmoke, Bewitched, Leave It to Beaver*, and *Candid Camera*. By the end of the decade, TV became much edgier, influenced by the political tumult of the era. Viewers of *Rowan & Martin's Laugh-In* and *The Smothers Brothers Comedy Hour* could count on seeing cutting satire that attacked the politicians of the era as well as some of the bedrock institutions that guided American life.

Tom and Dick Smothers were popular folk singers and comedians when their TV variety show premiered on the CBS television network in 1967. Instead of wholesome family entertainment, CBS executives soon found the show providing amusing sketch comedy about drug use and hippie culture. A regular feature on the show was the "Share a Little Tea with Goldie" segment starring comedienne Leigh French, who lampooned daytime TV talk shows. Portraying the character Goldie O'Keefe, French played the role as an airheaded hippie girl who seemed to be hosting her show while high on marijuana. (At the time, "tea" was a hippie term for marijuana.) Another regular character was Officer Judy, portrayed by comedian Bob Einstein. A no-nonsense policeman, Officer Judy invariably settled all disputes by spraying his antagonists in their faces with mace, a chemical used by police to subdue rowdy antiwar demonstrators.

Meanwhile, the show regularly lampooned conservative politicians, and the Smothers's guests were often the most popular rock stars of the era. Each week, the show pushed the boundaries of what CBS believed was acceptable content for prime-time viewing. Finally, in 1969 CBS canceled the show.

No Longer Taboo

More so than TV, the movies of the era tested the boundaries of what had for years been regarded as taboo content. In the early part of the decade, such films as *The Longest Day* and *The Great Escape* were released—both tell the stories of heroic World War II events. *Mary Poppins*, *The Music Man*, *The Sound of Music*, and *West Side Story*, popular musicals filmed in the early 1960s, scored hits at the box office.

As the decade progressed, though, films became edgier and more explicit in their content, offering audiences scenes of nudity, profanity, and violence. Films such as *Easy Rider*, *Midnight Cowboy*, *Bob & Carol & Ted & Alice*, *The Graduate*, *Bonnie and Clyde*, and *I Am Curious (Yellow)*, proved to be enormously successful, but their explicit content and examination of sensitive social issues prompted Congress to question whether laws would be needed to ensure that young children were not exposed to graphic content. Threatened with congressional action, the film industry acted on its own. In 1968 the Motion Picture Association of America (MPAA), the trade association of Hollywood studios, created a ratings code that helped guide parents and theater owners in deciding whether films would be appropriate for young children and teens. The ratings of G, M, R, and X were established, but they would eventually be refined to G, PG, PG-13, R, and NC-17.

The political issues of the day were also displayed on the stage and screen. *Failsafe* examines a nuclear confrontation between the United States and Soviet Union. So does *Dr. Strangelove*, but in a humorous context. *The Boys in the Band*, which was produced as an off-Broadway play in 1968, examines the lives of gays and was later adapted into a film. The Broadway musical *Hair*, a smash hit in 1968, tells the story of

The story of a young man who falls in with a freewheeling band of hippies and draft dodgers captured the spirit of the times in the hit Broadway musical Hair. *Several of the play's songs became anthems of the antiwar movement.*

a young man on his way to a military induction center who falls in with a freewheeling band of hippies and draft dodgers. The film *M*A*S*H* tells the story of rebellious army doctors serving during the Korean War, but its antiwar message resonated with an American public demanding an end to the war in Vietnam.

The New Culture

In the early years of the decade, thousands of teenage fans clamored to see the Beatles sing songs of romance while hit movies often portrayed bikini-clad teenagers having fun on the beach or soldiers bravely risking their lives for the cause of democracy. By the end of the decade, American popular culture was vastly different. The Beatles and other rock stars were now singing about peace and drug use. Books and films contained explicit content that a decade before would never have been available for public consumption. But judging from the long lines outside the theaters or the brisk sales of *Tropic of Cancer* and other popular books of the era, Americans had decided for themselves that controversial issues and explicit content should no longer be kept behind locked doors. The 1960s reflected the birth of a new American culture—a culture in which people no longer were bound by the conservative principles of the past.

Chapter 6

What Is the Legacy of the 1960s?

In June 1971, with war still raging in Vietnam, the *New York Times* commenced publication of a series of articles based on a secret study written by analysts at the Pentagon. Known as the Pentagon Papers, the documents shed new light on the American military's conduct of the war. Moreover it revealed that top officials in the government opposed American involvement in Vietnam, believing the conflict unwinnable. Among the comments reported by the Pentagon Papers were those of CIA director John McCone, who told President Johnson in 1964, "We will find ourselves mired down in combat in the jungle in a military effort that we cannot win, and from which we will have extreme difficulty extricating ourselves."[37] According to the *Times* stories, Johnson ignored McCone's advice as well as the misgivings about the war from his top military advisers. The *Times* story said Johnson planned to escalate the war months before the Gulf of Tonkin incident gave him cause to claim American vessels had been attacked by the North Vietnamese.

Nevertheless, for years Johnson and his successor, Richard M. Nixon, believed the war was winnable, choosing to ignore top military leaders and other advisers. Soon after taking office, Nixon ramped up the bombing of North Vietnam, but the North Vietnamese proved as resilient as ever. "They'll turn their collars up around their ears, pull in their necks, and ride it out,"[38] McCone predicted years before.

Nixon understood the effect the Pentagon Papers would have on American society. He told his chief aide, H.R. Haldeman, that he did not believe most Americans would understand the intricacies of American foreign policy exposed by the Pentagon Papers, but most people would nevertheless start viewing what they were told by their national leaders with skepticism. "To the ordinary guy, all this is a bunch of gobbledygook," Nixon told Haldeman. "But out of the gobbledygook comes a very clear thing: you can't trust the government; you can't believe what they say; and you can't rely on their judgment."[39]

For a war that was already unpopular, publication of the Pentagon Papers helped open new debates about the justification for continuing the fight. Nixon finally concluded that he would be unable to achieve a military victory. After winning commitments from the Chinese and Soviets that they would not arm or supply the North Vietnamese or Vietcong, in 1972 he announced plans for a withdrawal of US troops. The last American troops left Southeast Asia in the spring of 1973.

The Fall of Saigon

Without support of American troops, the South Vietnamese proved themselves ineffective fighters. It took just two years for North Vietnamese troops to make their way to Saigon. On April 29, 1975, scenes of chaos were broadcast on American TV as US military helicopters evacuated some one thousand American diplomats and six thousand Vietnamese citizens, mostly South Vietnamese government officials and their families who feared for their lives if forced to remain. A day later, Communist troops rolled into the city. Saigon was renamed Ho Chi Minh City (in honor of Ho, who died in 1969). Upon arriving in Saigon, North Vietnamese Army colonel Bui Tin told the citizens of the now united country, "You have nothing to fear. Between Vietnamese there are no victors and no vanquished. Only the Americans have been beaten. If you are patriots, consider this a moment of joy. The war for our country is over."[40]

Since 1955, when the first American military advisers arrived in Vietnam, 57,957 American troops had lost their lives in the war. Moreover, an estimated 2 million citizens of North Vietnam and South Vietnam—10 percent of the two countries' populations—were killed during the war. In addition to the toll the war had taken on human life, the war also left a tremendous black mark on the credibility of the

Five decades after the Civil Rights Act prohibited discrimination on the basis of gender, women have made only modest advances in their career paths and their paths into the halls of power in American government. In American politics, women have been all but frozen out of key leadership positions.

With few exceptions—such as California representative Nancy Pelosi's four-year term as speaker of the US House of Representatives—women have largely failed to achieve influential roles in political office. By 2012 just 73 of the 435 seats in the House and 17 of the 100 seats in the Senate were held by women. And while then–US senator Hillary Clinton made a serious run for the presidency in 2008, she ultimately fell short of winning her party's nomination.

Clinton, who went on to serve as secretary of state in the administration of President Barack Obama, is, however, widely expected to run for president again in 2016. Meanwhile, the gains of women on the US Supreme Court have been modest. In 1960 there were no women serving among the nine members of the nation's highest court; by 2012 just three women were on the court.

American government. No longer would Americans be so willing to trust their national leaders.

The legacy of Vietnam—that presidents and other national leaders cannot be trusted—has endured into the twenty-first century. Indeed, contemporary polls consistently show that a large proportion of Americans do not believe what they are told by their national leaders. In 1972 a Gallup poll reported that 73 percent of Americans said they trusted the president. In 2011 a Gallup poll found that just 47 percent of Americans trust the president—a statistic that may have been attributable in some measure to the declassification of Pentagon documents in 2008 indicating that the *Maddox* may not have been attacked in the Gulf of Tonkin, after all. The documents suggest that while North Vietnamese boats were in the vicinity, they may not have fired torpedoes at the American vessel, and that Johnson may have blown the incident out of proportion in order to garner support for the war.

New Strategy for War

In the wake of Vietnam, political leaders would adopt a new strategy for waging war: Presidents realized they would have to make a strong case to the American public before committing troops to action in a hostile nation. A key component of that case includes the assertion that the enemy represents a threat to American security, and troops should be committed only after negotiations seeking a peaceful resolution have failed. Under this policy, American troops would not be sent abroad to fight a proxy war in a country that poses no threat to America.

That policy was first enunciated in 1991 by Colin Powell, chairman of the US Joint Chiefs of Staff and later secretary of state under President George W. Bush. In what has been labeled the "Powell Doctrine," Powell, who served in Vietnam as a US Army major, also declared that when America would launch a military strike, it would do so with decisive and overwhelming resources to ensure the conflict would end quickly. That doctrine was applied in 1991 when Iraq invaded neighboring Kuwait, threatening American energy security because of the huge amounts of oil exported through the Persian Gulf by the tiny Arab kingdom and its neighbors. Adhering to the Powell Doctrine, President George H.W. Bush initiated Operation Desert Storm, driving the Iraqis out of Kuwait in a matter of weeks. But once the Iraqis left Kuwait, Bush called off the attack. Fearing a long conflict that could cost many American lives, Bush refused to remove the Iraqi dictator Saddam Hussein from power.

Since establishment of the Powell Doctrine, some presidents have been careful to follow its principles. When faced with international crises they seek to avoid committing American troops to long and weary conflicts. In 1995 President Bill Clinton refused to commit ground troops to the civil war in the former Yugoslavia, although—as a member of the North Atlantic Treaty Organization (NATO)—the US military did participate in air strikes to help end the massacre of civilians by Serbian troops and their allies. And in 2012 President Barack Obama refused to commit ground troops to help rebels overthrow Libyan dictator Mu'ammar Gadhafi but authorized air cover for the rebels, which ultimately did help bring down the Gadhafi regime.

In 2003 Clinton's successor, George W. Bush, did not adhere to the principles of the Powell Doctrine when he committed troops to ousting Saddam Hussein. According to Patrick Hagopian, an historian at Lancaster University in Great Britain, Bush violated the Powell Doctrine by committing far fewer troops than were necessary to maintain the peace in Iraq. Moreover, Bush claimed evidence had surfaced indicating Saddam possessed weapons of mass destruction—which therefore posed a threat to America and its allies in the Middle East. Citing this evidence, Bush forged a coalition of nations to invade Iraq and oust Saddam. At first, the mission was expected to take just a few weeks or months, but American troops ultimately spent seven years in Iraq. American troops suffered nearly five thousand deaths while some thirty thousand were wounded in the effort to keep the peace and install a Western-style democracy. And in the end, no weapons of mass destruction were uncovered. "The Bush administration indulged in an ambitious nation-building exercise unrealizable by military means," says Hagopian. "All of these features of the invasion repudiated the doctrine associated with Powell, secretary of state at the time."[41] In the years since the invasion, it became clear that Bush relied on scant evidence to make his case for war. Once again, US troops were fighting on foreign soil against an enemy who posed no threat to American security.

Modern Relations with Vietnam

America's invasion of Iraq caused deep divides in the Middle East and other corners of the globe as many nations have grown suspicious of

American intentions. But one country that enjoys healthy diplomatic relations with the United States is, ironically, Vietnam. Still under a Communist regime, the country has nevertheless made its peace with America. Although relations remained icy for several years after the war, in time diplomatic channels were reopened, and in 1993 Clinton removed trade barriers with Vietnam. Two years later the US State Department reopened its embassy in the Vietnamese capital.

A nighttime view of modern Ho Chi Minh City and its radiant skyline illustrates the distance Vietnam has traveled in the decades since the end of the Vietnam War. The country has seen dramatic growth in its economy and improvement in its standard of living.

Vietnam and America cooperate in a number of diplomatic initiatives, including joint campaigns to stem the flow of narcotics out of Southeast Asia. Vietnam has also cooperated with the US government in installing radiation detection equipment in the southern port city of Cai Mep–Vung Tau to help identify terror plots that would employ nuclear weapons.

In the years since America resumed trade with Vietnam, the Asian country has seen its economy expand and the standard of living for its citizens improve. America and Vietnam are trading partners, buying and selling some $20 billion worth of goods from one another each year. Vietnam exports clothing, shoes, furniture, leather goods, and nuts to America. Major American exports to Vietnam include automobiles, cotton, and industrial and farm machinery. Before normalization of relations between America and Vietnam, most Vietnamese workers earned the equivalent of $2 a day, or about $730 a year. In 2011, the Vietnamese government reported, the average Vietnamese worker earned about $2,200 a year. According to the World Bank, the Washington, DC–based financial institution that provides economic aid to developing countries, Vietnamese citizens enjoy a lower middle-class standard of living. In other words, in just two decades Vietnam has transformed itself from a country mired in poverty to a country with an industrial base and growing standard of living for its citizens. "This is one of the most impressive records of poverty alleviation in world history," a Western diplomat told *Atlantic* magazine journalist Robert D. Kaplan. "They have gone from bicycles to motorcycles."[42]

Accomplishments in Space

One former Vietnamese citizen who has flourished in American society is Eugene H. Trinh. His family left Vietnam in 1968, well before the fall of Saigon. Trinh attended college in America, earned degrees in physics, and eventually joined NASA's astronaut corps. In 1992 Trinh participated in a mission aboard the space shuttle *Columbia*, becoming the first Vietnamese American to fly in space.

In the years following the 1969 moon landing, the flights of the space shuttle emerged as the predominant NASA program, replacing

Cuba in the Twenty-First Century

The legacy of the Cuban missile crisis is reflected in the low standard of living in the island nation. Cut off from trade with America following the 1962 incident, Cuba seems frozen in the era. Cubans continue to drive 1960s-era automobiles, which they somehow keep running with a measure of mechanical ingenuity. One clever Cuban told *Philadelphia Inquirer* reporter Peter Mandel, who visited Havana, that he obtained a 1980s-era Lada, a car manufactured in Russia. "When I buy the Lada," the Cuban said, "the back of it was crushed. What do I do? I find one crushed in front. I weld them together."

Old-style rotary telephones are also common in Cuba. Many buildings in Havana and other cities remain in disrepair because Cuba lacks building supplies; as such, building walls are crumbling because of their constant exposure to the salt air of the Atlantic Ocean. Says Mandel, "Not one single soul, as far as I can tell, is texting, starting a phone call, or staring downward at an electronic device."

Quoted in Peter Mandel, "Time Trip to Cuba," *Philadelphia Inquirer*, July 29, 2012, pp. N1, N4.

manned spaceflight to the moon. After the 1969 landing by Neil Armstrong and Edwin "Buzz" Aldrin, another ten astronauts walked on the moon—the last team visiting in 1972.

Soon after the final flight to the moon, the American manned space program shifted into the space shuttle program, featuring a craft that was not designed to leave Earth's orbit. In 2012 the final space shuttle mission was launched, temporarily ending American sponsorship of manned spaceflight. Still, even though NASA has turned to other projects, the American space agency has accomplished many important achievements. NASA has sent unmanned satellites to Mars, some of which have landed on the planet's surface, conducting scientific experiments while transmitting vivid pictures of the Martian surface back to Earth. A 2012 mission to Mars sent a robot landing craft known as *Curiosity*; part of the rover's mission is to search for evidence of extinct life. Unmanned satellites have also been sent on fly-by missions to other planets, including Venus, Jupiter, and Saturn. In 1990 a space shuttle mission delivered the Hubble Space Telescope into Earth orbit, giving astronomers views of distant stars and planets impossible from ground-based telescopes. Hubble can provide these views because its lenses are not clouded by Earth's atmosphere. In 2011 NASA scientists announced that Hubble identified a galaxy some 13.2 billion light years from Earth. (A light year represents the distance traveled by a source of light in a single year, about 5.8 trillion miles [9.3 trillion km].) And in 2106 NASA expects to resume manned spaceflight.

The Struggle for Equality Continues

NASA also helped further the cause of civil rights when it accepted African Americans into the astronaut corps; the first African American to fly in space was Guion Bluford, who participated in a space shuttle mission in 1983. Certainly, Bluford's path to space was helped along by the accomplishments of the civil rights movement of the 1960s, but perhaps no person exemplifies the legacy of the civil rights movement more than Barack Obama, the forty-fourth president of the United States. Americans elected their first African American president in 2008—some five decades after the Freedom Rides, the Greensboro Four, James Meredith, and Martin Luther King Jr. made their mark on US history.

Obama's election proved that African Americans have achieved a measure of racial equality; many Americans, including women, believe they are still waiting to see the promise of equality fulfilled. When Betty Friedan published *The Feminine Mystique* in 1963, women made up just 38 percent of the workforce, and few of them held jobs in which they enjoyed a measure of authority—particularly over men.

The plight of women has improved over the decades, but many women still believe they are trapped below a glass ceiling. According to the US Labor Department, women made up 47 percent of the American workforce in 2010; however, the agency also reported that, on average, their salaries were 19 percent lower than salaries paid to men. Moreover, a 2011 study by the publication *International Business Reports* found that women hold just 15 percent of senior management positions at American corporations.

The Right to Protest

Perhaps the most important legacy of the 1960s is the realization by Americans that if they oppose an action by their government, they have the right to take to the streets in protest. Many people witnessing the so-called Occupy Wall Street movement of 2011 and 2012 recognized the influence of the 1960s antiwar demonstrations. In the Occupy protests thousands of people who felt American tax laws and other economic measures favor the rich camped out in public squares and refused to move until the leaders of their government took notice. When police were forced to move in and forcibly remove the protesters, images of demonstrators tangling with police were reminiscent of the street battles fought during the Vietnam War era.

Paul Friedman participated in protests against the Vietnam War. He also campaigned for civil rights for African Americans. In 2011, at the age of sixty-four, Friedman joined the Occupy Wall Street movement in New York City, which staged a two-month occupation of the city's Zuccotti Park. "I felt in my gut very much like what I was a part of in the 1960s,"[43] Friedman says.

Many members of the Occupy movement say they do not believe change will happen overnight—that it could take years before political leaders make the wealthy carry a larger share of the tax burden. Still, they intend to keep up the pressure on politicians—just as the students and other young people of the 1960s kept up the pressure on politicians to end the Vietnam War. Eventually public sentiment turned in their favor, and government leaders knew they had to find a way to bring

Angered by economic inequality and corporate greed, Occupy Wall Street protesters march in New York City in 2011. The modern protest movement in some ways reflects lessons learned during the 1960s.

American troops home. Indeed, by 2012, as the Occupy movement made daily headlines, numerous polls showed widespread support for raising taxes on the wealthiest 1 percent of Americans. "Politicians have to be pushed. You cannot just hope they will do the right thing,"[44] says Georgetown University history professor Michael Kazin.

The 1960s proved to be a turbulent time in American history. The decade was marked by war and tense race relations. But the accomplishments of the space program also showed that Americans could work together to achieve great things. As America moves further into the twenty-first century, its leaders would do well to look back to the events of the 1960s from time to time. A look back at those tumultuous times could help them avoid the mistakes of the past but take advantage of the tremendous energy that people brought to bringing about the changes that continue to guide American society today.

Source Notes

Introduction: The Defining Characteristics of the 1960s

1. William D. Ehrhart, *Vietnam-Perkasie: A Combat Marine's Memoir*. New York: Kensington, 1983, p. 18.
2. William D. Ehrhart, "Where [Have] All the Vietnam War Warriors Gone?" *National Catholic Reporter*, September 9, 1994, p. 15.
3. Quoted in *Progressive*, "Sure We Were Young," April 2009, p. 102.

Chapter One: What Conditions Led to the 1960s?

4. Quoted in Rita Giordano, "A New Boomer Era," *Philadelphia Inquirer*, December 19, 2005, p. 1.
5. David Halberstam, *The Fifties*. New York: Villard, 1993, pp. ix–x.
6. Halberstam, *The Fifties*, p. ix.
7. Quoted in Thomas Doherty, "The Army-McCarthy Hearings," Museum of Broadcast Communications, 2012. www.museum.tv.
8. Quoted in Doherty, "The Army-McCarthy Hearings."
9. Halberstam, *The Fifties*, p. 557.
10. Bob Dylan, "The Times They Are A-Changin,'" song, 1963. www.bobdylan.com.

Chapter Two: The Pursuit of American Exceptionalism

11. Quoted in David Greenberg, "Rewinding the Kennedy-Nixon Debates," *Slate*, September 24, 2010. www.slate.com.
12. Theodore H. White, *The Making of the President 1960*. New York: HarperCollins, 2009, p. 289.
13. Quoted in Tom Wolfe, *The Right Stuff*. New York: Farrar, Straus and Giroux, 1979, p. 72.
14. Quoted in Robert Dallek, *Flawed Giant: Lyndon Johnson and His Times*. Oxford, UK: Oxford University Press, 1998, p. 418.

15. Quoted in John Noble Wilford, *We Reach the Moon*. New York: Bantam, 1969, p. 80.

16. Quoted in Wilford, *We Reach the Moon*, p. 11.

17. Quoted in Harry Hurt III, *For All Mankind*. New York: Atlantic Monthly Press, 1988, p. 168.

18. Quoted in Hurt, *For All Mankind*, p. 176.

19. Quoted in Sybille Bedford, "Violence, Froth Sob Stuff—Was Justice Done?," *Life*, March 27, 1964, p. 32.

Chapter Three: Vietnam

20. Quoted in Stanley Karnow, *Vietnam: A History*. New York: Penguin, 1984, p. 327.

21. Quoted in L. Fletcher Prouty, *The Secret Team: The CIA and the Allies in Control of the United States and the World*. New York: Skyhorse, 2008, p. 233.

22. Karnow, *Vietnam*, p. 347.

23. Quoted in Hedrick Smith, "Westmoreland Says Ranks of Vietcong Thin Steadily," *New York Times*, November 22, 1967, p. 1.

24. Quoted in Thomas Hauser, *Muhammad Ali: His Life and Times*. New York: Simon & Schuster, 1991, p. 145.

25. Quoted in Brian Sulkis, "Conscientious Objector/Writer David Harris—Who Went to Prison for His Beliefs About the Vietnam War—Talks About the Forces That Shaped Him and the High Price of Loving Other People," *San Francisco Chronicle*, April 9, 1995, p. 3Z1.

26. Abbie Hoffman, *Soon to Be a Major Motion Picture*. New York: Berkley, 1982, p. 180.

27. Hoffman, *Soon to Be a Major Motion Picture*, p. 175.

Chapter Four: The Fight for Social Justice

28. Quoted in Larry Copeland, "Sit-Ins Reignited the Civil Rights Movement 50 Years Ago," *USA Today*, February 1, 2010. www.usa today.com.

29. Quoted in Joan Morrison and Robert K. Morrison, eds., *From Camelot to Kent State: The Sixties Experience in the Words of Those Who Lived It*. New York: Random House, 1987, p. 29.

30. Quoted in David Farber and Beth Bailey, *The Columbia Guide to the 1960s*. New York: Columbia University Press, 2001, p. 17.

31. Quoted in *Huffington Post*, "I Have a Dream Speech," January 17, 2011. www.huffingtonpost.com.

32. Betty Friedan, *The Feminine Mystique*. New York: W.W. Norton, 2001, p. 57.

33. Linda Lear, introduction to *Silent Spring*, by Rachel Carson. New York: Houghton Mifflin, 2002, p. x.

Chapter Five: Birth of a New American Culture

34. Quoted in Official Ed Sullivan Site, "The Beatles," 2010. www.edsullivan.com.

35. Neil A. Hamilton, *The 1960s Counterculture in America*. Santa Barbara, CA: ABC-CLIO, 1997, p. 148.

36. Robert L. Levey, "Friendly Fifty on Fort Hill—Better Way for People?," *Boston Globe*, December 12, 1967, p. 2.

Chapter Six: What Is the Legacy of the 1960s?

37. Quoted in CNN, "The Pentagon Papers: The Secret War," 1996. www.cnn.com.

38. Quoted in CNN, "The Pentagon Papers: The Secret War."

39. Quoted in Daniel Ellsberg, *Secrets: A Memoir of Vietnam and the Pentagon Papers*. New York: Penguin, 2003, p. 413.

40. Quoted in John S. Bowman, ed., *The Vietnam War Almanac*. New York: Barnes & Noble, 2005, p. 345.

41. Patrick Hagopian, *The Vietnam War in American Memory: Veterans, Memorials and the Politics of Healing*. Amherst: University of Massachusetts, 2009, p. 423.

42. Quoted in Robert D. Kaplan, "The Vietnam Solution," *Atlantic*, June 2012, p. 62.

43. Quoted in Mark Egan and Ben Berkowitz, "Insight: Occupy Wall Street, the Start of a New Protest Era?," Reuters, October 7, 2011. www.reuters.com.

44. Quoted in Egan and Berkowitz, "Insight."

Important People of the 1960s

Neil Armstrong and Edwin "Buzz" Aldrin: The two American astronauts set foot on the moon on July 20, 1969, fulfilling President Kennedy's mandate in 1961 to land men on the moon by the end of the decade. Armstrong and Aldrin were the first of twelve Americans to walk on the moon.

The Beatles: John Lennon, Paul McCartney, George Harrison, and Ringo Starr revolutionized rock 'n' roll in America, first appearing on *The Ed Sullivan Show* in 1964. Their long floppy hair set a style for American teenagers while their music turned from songs about romance to harder-edged music about drugs and antiwar themes.

Fidel Castro: A Communist, Castro seized power in Cuba on January 1, 1959. He successfully defeated a Central Intelligence Agency–sponsored insurrection against him at the Bay of Pigs, which convinced the dictator to seek protection from the Soviet Union. Cuba remains on unfriendly terms with America. Castro retired as president in 2008, but his younger brother Raul remains in power.

Chicago Seven: Activists Abbie Hoffman, Jerry Rubin, Tom Hayden, Rennie Davis, David Dellinger, John Froines, and Lee Weiner were charged with inciting the riots at the Democratic National Convention in 1968. Their trial the following year illustrated the deep divisions in American society among those who favored and opposed the Vietnam War.

Betty Friedan: Friedan's 1963 book *The Feminine Mystique* touched off the feminist movement in America as she reported the dissatisfaction of many women unable to pursue professional careers. Friedan's book sparked activism that resulted in laws guaranteeing gender equality, although five decades after its publication women are still striving for workplace equality.

Greensboro Four: Joseph McNeil, Ezell Blair Jr., David Richmond, and Franklin McCain sparked opposition to the Jim Crow laws of the South when they sat down at a whites-only lunch counter in Greensboro, North Carolina, on February 1, 1960. Refused service, the four African Americans remained at the counter for hours. Soon, thousands of other activists joined them in occupying whites-only sections of restaurants.

Ho Chi Minh: Ho emerged as the Communist leader of North Vietnam in the years following World War II and led the guerilla campaign that ousted the French in 1954. But when South Vietnamese leaders refused to participate in a 1956 election to unify the country, Ho declared war on the South and supported the South Vietnamese guerilla movement known as the Vietcong. Ho died in 1969.

Lyndon B. Johnson: Succeeding John F. Kennedy as president, Johnson pushed for landmark civil rights legislation to grant equality to African Americans and other minorities. But he also ramped up the Vietnam War, perhaps even faking the Gulf of Tonkin incident. As public opinion turned against the war, Johnson, fearing he would lose at the polls, chose not to run for reelection in 1968.

John F. Kennedy: Taking office as president in 1961, Kennedy proposed a New Frontier in which America would lead the world in civil rights, science, and all human endeavors. His main diplomatic success was forcing the removal of the Soviet Union's nuclear weapons from Cuba in October 1962. Kennedy was assassinated by a gunman while visiting Dallas, Texas, on November 22, 1963.

Martin Luther King Jr.: An organizer of the Montgomery bus boycott in 1955, King soon emerged as the nation's most influential civil rights leader. He led a civil rights march on Washington in 1963, delivering his "I Have a Dream" speech to a crowd of more than two hundred thousand. On April 4, 1968, while supporting sanitation workers in Memphis, Tennessee, King was assassinated by racist James Earl Ray.

Timothy Leary: The former Harvard University professor promoted the use of lysergic acid diethylamide, also known as LSD or acid, a mind-altering drug that often causes hallucinations. Leary left Harvard after giving drugs to students, spending the next several years living off the benevolence of friends and collecting fees for giving speeches.

Richard M. Nixon: Elected president in 1968 by assuring the voters he had a secret plan to end the Vietnam War, Nixon instead ramped up the bombing of the North. The North Vietnamese withstood the bombings, though, and Nixon finally concluded that the war was unwinnable. In 1972 Nixon negotiated an American withdrawal. Vietnam fell to the Communists three years later.

Tom and Dick Smothers: The folk singers and comedians hosted *The Smothers Brothers Comedy Hour* from 1967 to 1969. CBS executives thought the brothers would provide wholesome family entertainment, but the show soon evolved into a forum for edgy comedy and music as well as political satire. CBS canceled the show after three seasons, finding its content too controversial for family tastes.

For Further Research

Books

Raymond Arsenault, *Freedom Riders: 1961 and the Struggle for Racial Justice*. Oxford, UK: Oxford University Press, 2012.

Richard Brownell, *Counterculture of the 1960s*. Farmington Hills, MI: Lucent, 2010.

Robert A. Caro, *The Passage of Power: The Years of Lyndon Johnson*. New York: Alfred A. Knopf, 2012.

Alex Cruden, ed., *Student Movements of the 1960s*. Farmington Hills, MI: Greenhaven, 2012.

John Robert Greene, *America in the Sixties*. Syracuse, NY: Syracuse University Press, 2010.

Michael Lang, *The Road to Woodstock*. New York: Ecco, 2010.

Mark Atwood Lawrence, *The Vietnam War: A Concise International History*. Oxford, UK: Oxford University Press, 2010.

Jeffrey A. Turner, *Sitting In and Speaking Out: Student Movements in the American South, 1960–1970*. Athens: University of Georgia Press, 2010.

Websites

American Experience: **Vietnam Online** (www.pbs.org/wgbh/amex /vietnam). Companion website to the PBS documentary *Vietnam: A Television History*. Visitors will find a timeline of the war as well as biographies of the major policy makers and military leaders for the United States, South Vietnam, and North Vietnam. The site also includes personal reflections by those who fought in the war.

Baby Boomers (www.history.com/topics/baby-boomers). Maintained by the History Channel, the website covers the history of the baby boom—the generation of Americans born in the twenty years following World War II. The site includes statistics about the baby boom and stories of how the "boomers" came of age in the 1960s as they took part in the civil rights movement, fought in Vietnam, and protested the war at home.

John F. Kennedy Presidential Library and Museum: Cuban Missile Crisis (www.jfklibrary.org/JFK/JFK-in-History/Cuban-Missile-Crisis .aspx). The Kennedy presidential library in Boston maintains this website dedicated to the story of the Cuban missile crisis. Students can find a history of the thirteen-day crisis, audio from radio broadcasts during the October 1962 event, and a day-by-day account of how the president reacted to the crisis. Maps and photographs from the era can also be accessed.

Nobel Prize: Martin Luther King Jr. (www.nobelprize.org/nobel_prizes /peace/laureates/1964/king-bio.html). For his work in the cause of civil rights, Martin Luther King Jr. was awarded the 1964 Nobel Prize for Peace. The official website of the Nobel Prize includes a biography of King, a text of the speech by Gunnar Jahn, chairperson of the Nobel Committee who presented the prize to King, and a video of the ceremony in which King accepted the award.

The Official Ed Sullivan Site: The Beatles (www.edsullivan.com/artists /the-beatles). The site provides a history of *The Ed Sullivan Show*, including a page devoted to the three appearances by the Beatles in 1964. The site provides a background of the Beatles' appearances, the songs they performed, and a video of the group's February 9, 1964, performance. Information about many of the other stars who appeared on Sullivan's popular show can be accessed as well.

The Sixties: The Years That Shaped a Generation (www.pbs.org/opb /thesixties). Maintained by PBS as a companion website to its documentary *The Sixties: The Years That Shaped a Generation*, the site examines the turbulent political scene in 1960s America. Visitors can access the text of an online chat with Daniel Ellsberg, the Defense Department analyst who released the Pentagon Papers that exposed many of the truths about the war.

The Top 10 Protest Songs from the 1960s (www.toptenz.net/top-10 -protest-songs-from-the-1960s.php). The website features a list of songs regarded as the most popular protest songs of the era in which the artists voiced their opposition to the Vietnam War and their support for civil rights. Visitors can watch videos of John Lennon performing "Give Peace a Chance" and Country Joe and the Fish performing the "I Feel Like I'm Fixin' to Die Rag," among others.

Woodstock (www.woodstock.com). The site is dedicated to the 1969 rock festival staged near Woodstock, New York, attended by some five hundred thousand music fans. The site contains a history of the festival, photographs of the performers, a list of the performers, and information about concerts staged in 1994 and 1999 to commemorate the twenty-fifth and thirtieth anniversaries of the original festival.

Index

Picture Credits

Cover: AP Images
Maury Aaseng: 36
AP Images: 30, 81
© Bettmann/Corbis: 25, 41, 55
© Tim Clayton/Corbis: 76
© Corbis: 15
Photofest Pictures: 69
© Sunset Boulevard/Corbis: 20
© Harvey L. Silver/Corbis
© Ted Streshinsky/Corbis: 63
Thinkstock.com: 6, 7
Steve Zmina: 49

About the Author

Hal Marcovitz is a former newspaper reporter and author of more than one hundred fifty books for young readers. His other title in the Understanding American History series is *The Roaring Twenties*. He makes his home in Chalfont, Pennsylvania.